TRAUMAS
TRANSFORMATION
GLORY &

---◆---

E. Vivienne Anderson, MS, CASAC

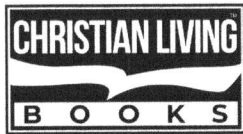

CHRISTIAN LIVING
B O O K S

Largo, MD

ISBN 9781562293840

Christian Living Books, Inc.
P. O. Box 7584
Largo, MD 20792
christianlivingbooks.com
We bring your dreams to fruition.

Printed in the United States of America

Dedication

This book is dedicated to the three most important strong and powerful men in my life: my sons and my grandson.

ENDORSEMENTS

Courage is not shown when we are forced to identify and acknowledge our deepest pain for the sake of our survival, but rather when we consciously choose to become "other-centered" enough to revisit our deepest pain and hurt by telling our story for the sake of providing hope to humanity. This book is the culminating work of E. Vivienne Anderson's journey from victim, victor, and to more than a conqueror. Thank you, Vivienne, for giving us a book that few others could have written. Every page reminds us that in- spite of how difficult our journey is, God has an ultimate plan and purpose for our lives.
This book is a must read for those who are called to give guidance on spiritual, personal, social or psychological problems.

Carol Dunn, MSCC
Educator and Christian Counselor

It is powerful to read about the transformative healing power of Jehovah-Rapha. A person who is hurting cannot help another person; because hurting people hurt people. Sister Vivienne Anderson's journey to wholeness and transformation qualifies her to speak into the lives of those who have been hurt and bring the transforming power of Jehovah-Rapha to cleanse and heal their wounds and open the doors to the abundant life in Jesus Christ. When God transforms the hurt into health the possibilities are endless!

Pastor A.W. Dees Sr. MPS
Holy Boldness Ministries COGIC

Foreword

Riveting!!! That's the word that keeps coming to mind after reading "Traumas, Transformation and Glory." Vivienne's story is powerful. It's a story of overcoming seemingly insurmountable odds. It's a story that offers hope to those who have been beaten down, abused, neglected, and forsaken in life. It's a story to bring healing to the broken-hearted.

Coming from a family with two loving parents, it's hard for me to imagine the horrors that Vivienne suffered growing up and that continued into her adulthood. And yet, somehow by God's grace and mercy, Vivienne has been transformed from victim to victor, from powerless to powerful, from needy to giving.

I personally know Vivienne and have had the privilege of watching part of her metamorphosis from caterpillar to butterfly, from rose bud to a beautiful flower. Vivienne lives her purpose to serve by BRINGING WHOLENESS, transforming spirit, soul, and body.

This book shares Vivienne's personal journey providing hope and encouragement to those who started with so little, yet somehow knows that life has much more to offer.

It's difficult to tell a story that requires recalling deep and painful wounds of the past, yet alone to share that with the masses. However, Vivienne has done so and in a masterful way.

I believe this book has the potential to save millions of babies from the death sentence of abortion, bring healing to millions of Moms who have experienced the nightmare of abortion, and restore many young girls and women who have been victimized by the sex trade.

As a former educator, a Marriage and Family Therapist, a New York Certified Alcohol Substance Abuse Counselor CASAC, Florida Certified Addictions Professional and someone trained in Therphostic Prayer Counseling, and Healing Traumas, Vivienne knows how to bring wholeness that transforms the spirit, soul, and body.

What this book offers the reader is wholeness, empowerment, and freedom. Without wholeness, it's difficult to be empowered. Without empowerment, it's difficult to find and maintain freedom.

Blessings to experience the healing and wholeness God desires for you!

Joseph Peck, M.D.

The Time Doctor

Author, *I Was Busy, Now I'm Not*

www.empower2000.com

P.S. It's possible for you to move from painful living to joyful living. Discover keys to let go of your sorrows and receive in exchange God's offer of "beauty for ashes, oil of joy for mourning, and the garment of praise for the spirit of heaviness" (Isaiah 61:3)!

PREFACE

It was never God's plan or thought for us to be traumatized or abused under any circumstances or in any situation by His original design. However, we live in a fallen world and bad things happen to the innocent and the good. Writing this book represents a journey back from a life riddled with traumatic events. Moving through traumas to wholeness and transformation is only possible through identification with the work of Jesus and His Cross. Despite all that life has handed me through the years, God gave me a glimmer of hope deep within that someday I would arise from the ash heap of dreams deferred to the joys of dreams fulfilled.

This book provides a background of my painful childhood and adult experiences. As a girl I grew up in a tropical paradise with a paternal grandmother who hated me for being alive and taking my father's attention away from her yet, she wanted me to follow in her ancestral path. Grammie once told me: "if I had known that your mother was pregnant with you, you would be dead." Growing up with her presented its challenges, but I managed to survive it all.

While I have made many poor choices in life, I learned from my mistakes and have become a strong, powerful woman of God today through the ministry of the Holy Spirit. God has been gracious, merciful, and faithful to me despite myself.

In my pursuit of an intimate relationship with my Heavenly Father, He has restored me from a life of shame to one of Dominion and being more than a conqueror. The essence of our Creator is love and He has lavished His love on me greatly. In the same manner, I make daily attempts to lavish my love back on Him because He loved me first. I love You Abba!

Acknowledgments

To my mother, thank you for giving me life. To the Johnson Clan, without all of you I would not be here. I have drawn from the deep well of strength in all of us during my darkest times, as well as the joyful times. I love you all. Miracles and favors without jealousy, envy, and coveting to all of us for a thousand generations of all our spiritual and biological seed!

I thank God for Aunt Inez, Mercella Johnson Francis who imparted the 23rd Psalm, and The Lord's Prayer into my spirit, which I also had to recite from memory when I was five years old.

To Aunt Inez and all the Johnsons who have always showed me love and acceptance. Thank you!

Special thanks to Steve and Pansy for their support and love that kept me walking when I felt like giving up on my health after the accident.

Pastor and Lady Dees thanks for your support during the "darkest nights of my soul."

Pastor and Lady Huggins thank you both and my Mt. Carmel family for being a part of my migration from the dessert of pain to the transforming elevation of wholeness.

Dr. Williams keep your Prayer Momentum going, it has been a great light during the dark nights of my soul.

To Apostle and Pastor Gayle Brown, Bread of Life thanks for Sunday nights refuge.

To Pastor McClurkin and the PFC Family I love you all! Grace, mercy, forgiveness and rich blessings.

To Brother and Sister Gordon, thank you for inviting me to church at First Assembly of God in Ocala Florida in August of 1987 where the love of God captured my heart.

To Pastor and Sister MacDaniel, thank you for your love support to me and my sons.

To my Sister Gayle you are a true and loyal sister in Christ. You have been there for me. Thanks!!!

To Minister Carol Cunningham thanks for the love, support, encouragement, and our praying sisterhood on my journey with this book.

To the Wyandanch Library staff thanks for your kindness. I love you guys!

Go Miss Dottie, Angie, and the awesome Literacy Volunteer team.

To the Upper Room Church-Deer Park, NY, thanks for being a place of healing for me. While I have moved on, I felt and still feel the love.

To my dear friend Melodie Lenny without whose help this book would not have its flow. Keep flowing *GIRL.*

Special Acknowledgment

Thank you Dr. Joseph Peck my life coach, mentor, and spiritual Dad for pouring your Holy Spirit gasoline into my life and this project. God brought you into my life at a time when I had given up on trusting spiritual leaders. Having a spiritual Dad is God's way of restoring one of the necessary good things in my life that had been missing for several years. Thank you for your encouragement and for the gentle ways that you help me to see my need to change my course of action and rediscover gift of having a positive attitude.

Thank you for being the "Time Doctor" and teaching me that wasting my time is wasting my life. You helped me to see how I could take back my power from those who tried to place their mind numbing limitations on who God said that I am. Thank you for inviting me to the "Awakening Conference" in August 2014 where the prophetic words that weekend changed my life and shifted my paradigm to fully embracing the pure prophetic word of truth.

Thank you for the hours you poured into me through coaching and the Dream Summit and praying with me. Thank you for helping to position me to embrace that, "I am a powerful woman of God." I believed it, but you were the first spiritual male authority in my life to proclaim me powerful in the universe. You gave me the All-important gift, of an earthly father's blessing when you proclaimed me "a powerful woman of God." Rich Blessings to you and Empower 2000, Inc.

CONTENTS

Breath of Healing

Breath of healing fall on me.
Breath of healing fall on me.
Breath of healing fall on me
And heal me till I hurt no more.
Salve of compassion wash me in Your Blood.
Cleanse my bitter traumatic wounds
And fill me with Your Love
Till all my pains are gone
And my soul is freed to love.
Heal me till I hurt no more.
Breath of healing fall on me.
Breath of healing fall on me.
Breath of healing fall on me.

© by E. Vivienne Anderson

INTRODUCTION

As a girl growing up in the tropical splendor of Jamaica, I suffered abuses and unbearable pain at the hands of my father, my grandmother and his family. One of the painful episodes in my childhood occurred after my mother kidnapped me and later returned me to my father because she could not financially provide for me. She sat on the steps of my father's apartment and promised me that she would come back for me, but before she could come back, my father sent me away to his mother in Montego Bay. Another more terrifying episode was when my father and his mother buried me alive upside down in a coffin one night in the woods. It was to terrify me into submission to the lawless ways of Satan and my grandmother's cult practices. I was only seven years old.

These abuses were so horrific that I developed an imaginary childhood friend which I affectionately named Charlotte. Later Crystal came along and they became my constant companions to help me cope as a child and later as an adult. It is to Charlotte and Crystal, my inner sisters, that I would often bare my soul. As an adult woman, I also experienced the pain of domestic violence, adultery, pornography, and abortion while I was married. After I shared these experiences with my close trusted friend; she said, "you need to write and publish your story." Her words were confirmation to me that I needed to begin my journey of becoming a writer. As a girl, I would dream about being a writer, but I never shared my dream with anyone.

Growing up alone not knowing who I was and feeling like a throw away child, the possibility of me becoming a writer was

19

an elusive dream. Writing seemed like an adventurous way to live. I would fantasize losing myself in books to forget the harsh, disruptive, and abusive cycles taking place in my life.

My parents were not able to put aside their personal difficulties with each other and see to my needs. They were disconnected from the realities of how I was growing up most of my life. I would sometime go for years without seeing either of them. My father did, however, send financial support to whoever I was living with throughout my childhood. It is only by the power and grace of God that I am alive and in my right mind today.

I am grateful to my mother's older sister, Aunt Inez, for making me memorize the Lord's Prayer and the 23rd Psalm when I was only five years old. I know that God placed Aunt Inez in my life to prepare me for what was to come. He knew that I would be abandoned by my parents, so He used Aunt Inez to establish His word in my heart first. This would prove crucial to my very survival during the years that my father was molesting me and after he sent me to Montego Bay to keep me and my mother away from each other.

The Lord Jesus Christ instructed me to share my life experiences in this book, knowing that I am not the only person to suffer such unbearable pain. This book is dedicated to all who have suffered and are suffering from any form of abuse. If it had not been for the Spirit of God protecting me, I would not have survived my past experiences. It is my earnest hope that those who have been hiding behind the many faces that masks the secrets of their abuses, will find hope as they journey through my life. If you have experienced verbal, sexual, emotional, physical, satanic ritual abuse, and or spiritual abuses, you will find solace that comes only through the person of Jesus Christ. He will heal you layer by layer of all the woundedness and brokenness of your past. He is the only one who can!

CHAPTER ONE

HUMBLE BEGINNINGS

I was born in Burnt Ground St. Elizabeth on the Island of Jamaica to an unmarried mother, Hazel Johnson and a married father, the late Leonard Constantine Hines. At the time of my conception, my mother was twenty-one years old. When my mother became pregnant with me, my father insisted she go back to her family in Burnt Ground near Santa Cruz and have the baby around her family. His real motive was to get my mother out of sight to hide her pregnancy from his wife and her well to do family. Prior to her leaving for the country, he gave her an engagement ring and asked her to marry him. My mother was excited to become engaged. What she did not know is that my father was married, and his wife was also pregnant with their third child.

When my mother returned to her family, she was not welcomed home. Pregnant without a husband, she was treated poorly. I am told my grandmother made this comment, "You're coming home to me with a 'Belly' and no husband?" My mother was already feeling ashamed and this comment only served to intensify her shame and released shame in my spirit while I was in her womb. While my mother was staying at her family's home, she received a letter from my father, late in her pregnancy, saying that his wife died in childbirth. He further stated in his letter that his mother, my grandmother, had killed his wife and their (3) babies with obeah/witchcraft using money that he sent to financially care for her. This is how my mother learned that she was carrying the child of a married man.

Shortly after my mother received this letter, she went into labor and I was born. Her mother was the attending midwife who delivered me and later my sister Rachel. I am told that during the labor and delivery my grandmother saw my forehead coming first through the birth canal rather than the top of my head. When she saw my forehead first, she said, "This is going to be a fierce child." My mother was expecting me to be a boy because my father wanted a boy to carry on his name. After I was born, my mother experienced what we now call post-partum depression which lasted some months. My father continued his financial support to her, so she was able to provide for us. My mother stayed in Burnt Ground with me and returned to Kingston when I was about six months old. However, by that time my father had a new companion named Edna who did not like me or my mother.

Pentecostal Beginnings

In Jamaica, Pentecostal services were sometimes held in the streets in their early days. There might have been some type of shack, store front, or tent where services were held inside on Sundays. The point of "street services" was to take the gospel to the streets to compel sinners to come Jesus. These street meetings were held at different places in Kingston wherever there was a light pole on the corner of the street. Pentecostals would clap their hands, beat tambourines, and play harmonicas or mouth organs and sometimes play a guitar. They were also called the "clap hands" people. My mother received Christ as her Savor at a street meeting in Jones Town after she returned to Kingston with me. At street services" there were no chairs to sit on and those were not the days of baby carriers.

My First Fire

It was to attend one of these street meetings that my mother left me one night with a friend in the rooming house where she lived in Jones Town. While she was at the street meeting, the friend who was babysitting me had a visit from her boyfriend. I was ten months old at the time and walking I was told. She took me while I was sleeping and put me to bed in my mother's room. I woke up and crawling around I was coming off the bed. Next to the bed was a table with a kerosene lamp on it. When I reached and grabbed the tablecloth, it pulled down the kerosene lamp which fell, broke, and started a fire. I began screaming and the babysitter and her boyfriend came and rescued me. I was burned on the inside of my left leg which caused a raised scar there for many years. It was decided after this incident of the fire that my mother was not responsible enough to care for me and an unofficial custody was given to my father who kept me during the days and my nights were spent at Aunt Inez her sister.

Kept from My Mother

My mother was not allowed to see me without my father's permission. However, Aunt Inez would allow her to visit with me often at her home without his knowledge. As I grew and became aware of the arrangements, I was asked to keep it a secret from my father that I saw my mother. This arrangement eventually leads, to very strained relationship between my mother and Aunt Inez for some years, but I was never told the details. However, I continued to be cared for by Aunt Inez and my father until I was old enough to attend a private day nursery at the Seventh Day Adventist Church she attended.

My father worked at nights, but he would come early in the mornings before Aunt Inez left for work. He would sit me on the handlebar of his bicycle and take me to day school beginning about age four. He would bring me snacks at recess and bring me home for lunch then take me back to school. Aunt Inez would pick me up from the Seventh Day Adventist Day School and I would spend my evenings with her and her son Stephen. This was the daily routine. When my father had his nights off from work, I would spend the nights with him at his house. The community's view of me was that I was a princess being treated very well by my father. No one looking at us from the outside would have been willing to believe or accept that my father could be sexually abusing me, his little princess.

Incest by My Father

I do not recall at what age my father began to perpetrate incest against me. My earliest memory of him sexually abusing me is about (3 or 4) three years old until my mother kidnapped me. At the time she kidnapped me I thought she took me from him because she knew he was molesting me, but I later learned I was mistaken. His girlfriend would spend some of her nights at my father's house. We all slept on the only double bed in a very large room that served as his apartment. There was a common bathroom and outdoor shower facility which everyone in the yard shared. Each household had a "chimmy" or a chamber pot that was used during the nights which had to be emptied and washed each morning. Bowel movements had to be held until morning to avoid the foul stench during the night. If it could not be held until morning you would have to go to the bathroom outside at night and it was dark.

My Father's Social Status

My father was a chef at University College Hospital and an excellent cook at home. He also had his private shoe making, shoe repairing business at home on our verandah. As a shoemaker my father would listen to someone describe the style of shoes they wanted, or they would show him the pattern in a magazine. From what he saw or heard he would draft the pattern and build the shoe from scratch. He took accurate measurements of men, women, and children's feet so their shoes would fit them perfectly. His goal for shoe making was that each pair shoe that he made fit well and lasted a long time. He provided well, he was very social able and well liked. He was also involved in the local political scene. He would work at polling stations and organize the teams that went out and canvased the community to register people to vote. He was a stanch supporter of the local political party and a sexual predator against his daughter all at the same time.

My Father's Cruelty

As a small girl my father did not tolerate any mistakes from me. I was beaten severely by him whenever his girlfriend Edna would complain. Edna never ran out of complaints against me, so I was beaten almost daily. Whenever I made a mistake in my schoolwork my father would hit me in my head with his knuckles. He also had a system of beating me. He kept an empty five-pound butter pan filled with water. In the butter pan of water, he kept a strip of leather about one inch wide and about eighteen inches long. I was told to lay across the bed. He would pull my dress over my head, pulled my underwear down and beat me on my bare bottom. I was ordered by him not to cry while he was beating me. If I cried, he would beat me longer until I would urinate on myself.

When my father learned that Aunt Inez was allowing my mother to see me. I accidently let it slip that I saw my mother. It started a quarrel between Aunt Inez and my father, which led to me being taken from Aunt Inez's care. I began to spend the nights alone at his apartment when I was about five years old. When I asked him why I could not spend the nights with Aunt Inez, "Your Aunt Inez cannot be trusted to keep your mother away from you, he said." His girlfriend Edna did not spend the nights at his apartment when he was at work she stayed at her own house and I was never sent to spend the nights at her house. I was left alone in the apartment after he molested me before he went to work at nights.

Recurring Nightmare

While I was spending the nights alone at my father's house, I recall having this recurring nightmare. In my nightmares there was always a light complexion black woman with long dark hair who was trying to slap my face. No matter how many times I woke up crying when I fell back to sleep, the same dream would be there waiting for me. Our neighbor Mrs. Robinson would come and take me into their apartment sometimes, but when my father learned of this, he stopped it. He and Mrs. Robinson quarreled over it and they did not speak to each other for some time.

My Mother's Hidden Visits

It was during those times when I was no longer staying with Aunt Inez that my mother began to come and visit me at his house. The first time that she walked into the yard and attempted to visit with me at his home he ran her out of the yard. She seemed to be afraid of him although, I never saw him hit her. His words to her was always harsh and angry and her words were cross and angry back at him. She would maintain a safe distance with her hand on her hip as she answered him back. He would chase her and tell her she was not fit to raise me because she left me to go to church. He would also tell her she was not good for anything. I used to feel he did not want her to see me because I was a bad child or that I must have done something wrong. Or that maybe I was also not good for anything like her.

I Had a Mouth Full of Sores

I became very ill with sores all over my mouth and a very high fever when I was about six years old. I became listless for days unable to eat with no desire to play. My father kept me home from school. Eventually he took me to my mother, and she stayed home from her job to take care of me for a while. I never learned what my illness was called that almost killed me. My mother took me to the University College Hospital which was a teaching facility with medical students and students from other Caribbean Islands. The doctor wanted to know why she had waited so long to bring me to the doctor and told my mother that if she had waited another day the illness would have spread into my lungs and I could have died. She made a sigh when she heard the doctor's words. I was living with my father who made me ill from molesting me, yet, she was being called a neglectful mother for my illness. I still recall my mother being kind and caring towards me at the time, but this would change when I encountered her again in later years.

Daily Hospital Visits for Shots

My mother took me to the doctor at University College Hospital every day for twenty-one days where I received injections each day and she was given a solution to paint all over my mouth with some type of washing solution. After the series of shots, I returned twice weekly for some time. Until I was only going monthly, when I was released, I could be returned to school and play with other children. Before this time, I was kept under quarantine and away from other children I stayed in my mother's room and was not allowed to play. While I liked to play, being kept inside is something I was familiar with. I was happy to be staying with her and they did not fight as much when I was sick. My father visited us every day. He never entered the room where we lived. We would both stand in the doorway and they would talk while he stood outside. He gave her money every day for food, to take us on the bus to and from the hospital, and to pay her rent. Sometimes he would bring food that he cooked when he came to see us. Most of the time he brought soup or porridge because I could not eat any solid food.

After I was well, they began to fight again because my mother felt that, I should be with her not return to live with my father alone. When it was time for me to return to school, my father came by one day walked in, packed all my clothes and took me with him. I did not want to go back with him, and I told her so, but he dragged me away from her with both of us crying as he placed me on the handlebar of his bicycle, and we rode out of the yard. One neighbor said, "What a wicked man taking the little girl from her mother after she nursed her back to health."

As we rode home on his bicycle, I continued crying. He warned me if I did not stop my foolishness, he would give me something to cry for when we got home. Remembering how he would beat me, I quickly dried up my tears. I don't know what we had for dinner that night, but he molested me again before he went to work that night. That night I had the nightmare again after he left. I used to feel like there was something wrong with me because of my parents' actions especially my father's actions against me and felt my mother was powerless to change anything. When I returned to the church school, everyone was happy to see me, and the other kids kept asking me if my father was bringing snacks at recess. He did and I shared some with them.

My Mother's Visits

After he dragged me away from my mother that day, I did not see her for a very long time. Then one day I heard a soft voice calling Vivienne, Vivienne. When I looked in the direction towards the June Plum Tree that was in our yard to the left of the gate, I saw my mother standing hidden behind the tree. I began to leave the verandah where my father was working on shoes. "Vivienne, who told you could go out and play?" "Daddy, a finish me lessons and I just want to go and see if any June Plum fell off the tree." "Ok, go." So, I walked down to the June Plum Tree and my mother was standing there in an orange floral dress with a belt around the waist. She put up her pointer finger over her mouth and told me to shush and I did. She pulled out a piece of brown paper and gave me a piece of her Bulla Cake.

I stood there and ate it all up, then my father called out, "Vivienne, if you didn't find any June Plum from under the tree by now, come back on verandah and sit your bottom on this bench." I said goodbye to my mother and ran back to the verandah and sat back down on the bench. My father did not allow me to be far out of his sights when he was around, I could only play when he was not around. "What it that you are eating", my father asked. "I found one June Plum", Daddy. All this time I was so filled with fear that if he found out I went to see my mother under the June Plum Tree, I would get a beating and she would be cursed out. I began to watch by the June Plum Tree every day and told Mrs. Robinson's nephew Selwyn that she was visiting me, but don't tell nobody.

Back to Santa Cruz

One day she came by the June Plum Tree and my father was not at home. I ran to her and she gave me another piece of her Bulla Cake. As I was eating my Bulla Cake, I looked down and she was barefoot. I had (3) pairs of shoes, one for yard, one for school, and one for church on Saturdays when Aunt Inez would come and take me to church with her. My mother had no shoes on her feet. My father the shoemaker did not care that the mother of his child had no shoes. Only that she stayed away from me. She knew that Aunt Inez would bring me to her house after Sabbath and I would spend the night. She told me she was going back to country. (Country: Jamaicans who are in Kingston call other parts of Jamaica the country or going to country.) Me can come with you. Can I come with you? She told me not to tell anybody we were going to country. Well my father made me swear not to tell her he was molesting me, or he would kill her. So now I would be keeping her secrets also.

All I knew is that we would be going to country. One Saturday, when I went to church with Aunt Inez, my mother came to her house and we had Sabbath meal with some of her other Adventist friends. My mother said she was taking me to the shop to buy me Paradise Plum candy or ("sweetie" as we used to call it) that I used to love. They were half red and half yellow covered with white granulated sugar. They were sweet with a lemony taste, they had an oval shape, and left my tongue red and tangy. When we left Aunt Inez we walked for a long time, but instead of going to get paradise plum sweetie, we walked from Trench Town to get a bus at the marketplace to Burnt Ground, Santa Cruz where she was from and where I was born.

I Was Afraid

I was frightened because I knew my father would be very cross that I left with her. Aunt Inez would be in trouble with him for letting her take me. Anyhow, after we got on the bus and I fell asleep and did not wake up until the bus stopped in Santa Cruz. When we got off the bus it was pitch black dark, and I heard country sounds of crickets and critters I had never heard before. My mother told me we were fine and not to be afraid. She held my hand tight and carried her bag with her belongings in her other hand. We walked from where the bus let us off in Santa Cruz to Burnt Ground in the dark where my grandmother Mary lived. I do not know how she found the path to walk to my grandmother's house because we had NO light.

When my mother came to Aunt Inez' house that day her belly was very big. I had never seen her belly that big before. Once back in Santa Cruz she was treated poorly again. My grandmother

Mary was vexed that her daughter was home once again pregnant without a husband. "Ruth, another belly and no husband! You can spend a few weeks here, but this time you cannot stay, not this time." After that my grandmother and mother did not speak much. My mother and I stayed in the extra room in the house my grandmother lived in. We slept on wooden bed next to the room my grandmother lived in. A few days after we got to Burnt Ground, Grannie told my mother to build a house on the clearing for herself and the children.

My Grandmother's Offer

My grandmother must have thought that her daughter Ruth was done looking for love outside herself. My mother went to a longtime friend who built a one room house for her with what money she saved and brought home with her. I heard him ask my mother to marry him one night. They were outside her house and thought I was asleep. She said this is not your "belly". He said, "I know, but I will raise the "belly" like my own. I also have another daughter in Kingston with her father's mother. We can go and get her from Kingston and raise them together." Still she said no! She said she was afraid that the woman he had children with might work obeah/witchcraft against her. However, it is more likely she felt she did not deserve a chance with him because of her past mistakes. He told her to send me to the dairy where he worked, and he gave us one quart of milk every day. I got up early in the morning to walk there and back. He would give me a cup of hot milk to drink before I took our quart of milk back to my mother for my sister. He seemed like a kind man and I did not feel afraid around him the way that I did with my father.

In addition to the one room house, he builds two wooden beds for us to sleep in. He also made a dining table and two chairs. My mother build shelves on the wall and build a wardrobe for clothes into the wall. The wardrobe had a piece of fabric draped around it with an opening slit in the middle to cover the clothes. The beds were made from sturdy boards and the mattress covers were made from burlap and stuffed with grass. We went all over our property and cut grass, then laid them out to dry in the sun.

The empty burlap bags came from the shop after the shopkeeper sold all the sugar the bags were washed and laid flat to dry.

Once the burlap bags were dried, we would cut them open and my mother showed me how to help her sew them together to make casing to be stuffed with grass as a mattress. The only problem with stuffing a mattress with grass is, the grass would stick out and poke me as I tried to sleep. However, I grew accustomed to it quickly and fell asleep easily after a few nights. It was not as good as the double bed in my father's house where I was being molested, but I was not afraid to go to sleep at nights. While I was in Burnt Ground, no one molested or raped me. We made two mattresses one for her bed and one for the bed me and my sister Rachel sleep in. We used a lot of grass to stuff the mattress and from time to time we had to get more grass and keep stuffing them because the grass got flat very quickly.

My grandfather Abel was dead by that time but before he died, he put my grandmother's name on the property's title. So, Mary Brown Johnson was the owner of the property left by Able Johnson. The room had two windows, a door, and a zinc roof with thatch. Whenever it rained outside, it also rained inside, and we would use pans and buckets to catch the water. Catching water in pans from the rain would save me a trip to the tank and later the well when the tank my grandfather built dried up to carry water. One of my chores in the country was to carry water for us to use. One day when I went to the tank to get water and I saw small snakes and frogs at the bottom of the concrete tank. I dropped my water bucket and ran crying. At that age my depth perception was too incomplete for me to understand that the snakes and frog could not climb out and bite me. Shortly after my mother went back home and the house was built, she had my sister Rachel. Once again, my grandmother was the midwife for her daughter when she went into labor with my sister Rachel. Looking back delivering her daughter's babies seemed to be the only closeness that my mother and grandmother shared with each other.

My Mother Resorted to Higglering

My mother became a haggler after my sister was born because we had very little money. She sold roasted peanuts, pimento/peppercorn, fruits, and other goods in the market. She did not make the money she wanted to make higglering, as it is called, to provide for us, but looking back there was a restless spirit in my mother. A haggler is a woman who sells produce, ground provisions and other goods in the marketplace to make her live and care for her children. It was around this time that my mother's attitude towards me changed. She was always cross or miserable and I felt the brunt of her misery sometimes. I was seven by then, too young to know why she was miserable but old enough to know she was not happy. My mother had written to my father, but he refused to provide any financial support for me which angered her and increased her financial misery. However, that Christmas he sent a package with three dresses and three pairs of shoes, socks, underwear and a white doll. Some member in the family was getting married so the dresses and shoes were divided out so that three of us could be flower girls in the wedding.

Mom Went Back to Kingston

We did not stay in Burnt Ground very long. My mother left me and my sister Rachel when she was still an infant with our Aunt Linda and Uncle Brownie who had children of their own. I recalled one day my grandmother Mary came into her daughter Linda's yard angry that Ruth has left her children with you and she's gone again. I did not understand what she meant, I only knew it did not feel good for us to be called "bastards" My grandmother Mary was not an uncaring woman, she was a good woman. She believed very strongly that men and women should be married before they begin having children. So, when her daughter Ruth now had her third daughter without being married it grieved her deeply and she made her feelings known. She was married to my grandfather Abel Johnson before she had her children and wanted the same for her children. Aunt Linda, Uncle Brownie, their children and all my other cousins in Burnt Ground were very kind to me and my sister. They never hit us the way my father's family did me when I went to Montego Bay. During the years that I was in Montego Bay I used to wish that my mother had left me in the country with her family. I believe that I would have been treated better by her family than I was with my father's family.

Mealtime at Aunt Linda and Uncle Brownie's was the same as when my mother was home. On Saturday's we usually had soup and there was some form of meat protein with our Sunday meal when they could afford it. When we had Rice and Peas it was very special because brown rice was a commodity in those days. I attended the all age school in Santa Cruz, but I did not like it there. The teacher I had was always very cross and the classes were large, so I felt lost. When I attended the church school in Kingston the classes were very small, and Sister Williams was not cross. One day I was late for school and the teacher hit me in my hand and I had a slight scratch on my wrist. My mother went to school the next day and spoke with the teacher about hitting and cutting me. The teacher never hit me again, and she complained that my mother had no right to come and speak to her about hitting and cutting me.

Back to My Father

My mother went back to Kingston after leaving us but returned a short while later to take us back with her. Once we were back in Kingston, my father came to where she was and put me on the handlebar of his bicycle and took me back to his house. When she brought me back to him, I felt that she took me back to him because she did not care about him molesting me. I never told her he was molesting me. I just thought that she knew he was and that is why she took me away from him. Shortly after my father came and took me back, he told me I would be going Montego Bay to live with his mother. The plans were already settled. It was after my mother came by my father's apartment and said she was getting a room for us. I don't know if my father overheard her, or if he had planned all along to send me away so that she could not find me.

Looking back, I wondered why he did not run her out of the yard that day. He told me he had written to his mother Grammie and she agreed to have her only granddaughter at the time come live with her. I had never met any of my father's side of the family, so I did not want to go and stay with her. As a seven-year-old girl I had no choices about where I went or where I stayed or about anything else

My First Suicidal Thought

After it was decided I was going to Montego Bay and a few days before I was to leave my father physically raped me. That was the first time that I wanted to kill myself after my father raped me when I was returned to him. Before that time, it was molestation, but he had not fully raped me. The next day I went somewhere with my Aunt Inez and as we were passing a bridge. I dropped back behind her and climbed up on the edge of the bridge, spread my arms out to my side and I began to think to myself, if I fall off this bridge and die, my father cannot send me away or hurt me anymore. However, before I could move my foot to lose my balance and fall, Aunt Inez grabbed me by my waist and pulled me down from the edge of the bridge. "Vivienne," she said, "That was very dangerous. Do not climb up there again." The thought of suicide did not leave me, and I would make many more attempts as the pain of my life increased throughout the years. Aunt Inez held my hand very firm as we walked the rest of the way. She never made any mention that she thought that I was trying to take my life.

Chapter Two

Growing up in Montego Bay

For the occasion of going to Montego Bay to live with his mother, my father bought me a Delcemina Grip which was small sturdy brown suitcase for my belongings. His live-in-girlfriend Edna made a new outfit for me. The woman he left my mother for was a dressmaker by trade, which was a thriving business in those days compared to my mother who was a domestic worker. She made my traveling outfit from lime green taffeta material and a fine soft lime green net to go over the taffeta. My father made me a pair of white leather shoes with a "T" strap up the middle with two side straps and flower designs cut all over the lower front of the shoe. I wore white socks that were folded at my ankles with my hair parted in two down the middle, platted and white bows on each side of my hair that had grown by then.

On the day that I was leaving for Montego Bay, my father woke me up early and made a breakfast of cornmeal porridge, with a slice of Hard Dough Bread with butter, and a fried egg. After we had breakfast my father took me to the bathroom and gave me a bath. (It did not feel right him bathing me when I was old enough and could give myself a bath). He dressed me, then we rode on his bicycle to the train station. He told me that the conductor would be-in-charge-of-me until I was met in Montego Bay later that day by his mother. I had been on a bus ride with my mother from Kingston to Santa Cruz when she kidnapped me, but this was my first train ride. I was alone and I was terrified, petrified, stupefied, and traumatized. I sat in total disbelief because I kept praying that this day would not come but here is was. My mother was not given any information that I was being sent away to his mother in Montego Bay, she found out after I was already gone

Train Conductor

The conductor of the train told me that I would be just fine. Easy for him to say he was a big grown up man like my father, I was a small girl. I was being sent to a place I was not known and where I knew no one. At least when my mother kidnapped me, I sort of knew her and her family was nice to me. The train conductor told me to let him know when I needed to go to the toilet. He did not say bathroom he said toilet. My father gave the conductor my ticket, a small sized white envelope which had money in it rather than instructions on how to care for me. He also gave the conductor money that was not in an envelope; and he kissed me on the forehead and left me sitting there all by myself. The conductor closed the doors and made his announcement about the train's destinations. Montego Bay in the Parish of St James was the last stop. (A parish is what we would call a state in America.) I began to cry as soon as the train began to move. I looked out the window, but I did not see my father for he already ridden away on his bicycle leaving me alone.

During the train ride I did not eat the meal my father made for me. It was a sandwich made of heated Bully Beef" or Canned Corn Beef with scallions on hard dough bread which was cold by then. Libby's Bully Beef of course, because in those days that was the only company that sold Bully Beef in Jamaica and a bottle of Cola Champagne soda. The name Bully Beef came from the picture of the red bull on the cover of the tin. Bully Beef is ground up Corn Beef which was very salty in those days. I sat motionless on the train. I was so afraid that I did not even tell the train conductor when I needed to use the toilet because I wanted to hold it in. Although the toilet seemed only a few feet away from me it was a very long mile to walk by myself. I just sat there and wet on myself. I felt glued to my seat on the train that day wishing the ride would never end.

My Arrival in Montego Bay

When we got to the Montego Bay Station the train pulled into the yard. I looked through the train window and saw a short grey-haired woman with a tie-head with my fathers' face. She asks the train conductor for me and he came onto the train and took me by the hand and walked out with me and my Delcemina Grip. He handed me over to her and gave her the small white envelope that my father gave him for her. He complained to her that he showed me where the toilet was, and I was a big enough girl to go to the toilet by myself. I was older enough to go by myself except that I was too terrified to move. She introduced herself to me as Grammie and told me that she was my father Leonard's mother. Grammie scolded me for wetting myself. I felt ashamed. I was not a bed wetter I only wet the bed when my father was beating me. I knew at our first meeting I did not like her. My spirit never took to her and she never took to me either.

When I got to where she lived, she gave me dinner. They ate dinner very early in the day and would have some fruits, baked foods like cornmeal pudding, sweet potato pudding cassava pone, Bulla Cake with lemonade or tea later in the evenings. Their house was bigger than where my father lived. They only lived in half of the house while the other half was rented out to two other couples.

Neither of the women worked or was married, and both had permanent living companions with no visible children. The couple in the back had violent quarrels with hitting, while the couple in the front had violent quarrels but no hitting. When it was time for bed, my grandmother told me I was sleeping under the bed. It had been decided before I arrived that I would be sleeping on the floor under Grammie, my grandmother's bed.

The following day I was told by Grammie what my purpose was for being there. "My father is paying for me to stay here", I said, at which point Grammie slapped me across my face and said, "shut your mouth, you are a child." I was around simply for my ability to perform chores Grammie and her daughter Mrs. Queen deemed beneath them to perform. My father paid them a monthly sum of money for my room and board to be their maid, yet he refused to financially provide when I was with my mother in the country.

I Was Treated Differently

For my breakfast on that first morning in Montego Bay, I was given a cup of "bush tea" no sugar and one slice of stale Hard Dough Bread without any butter or jam. My other cousins who lived with Grammie had boiled green bananas, fresh picked (Spinach) Callaloo from their garden with Salted Cod Fish. It was a weekday morning. This became the primary manner of how I was fed and treated differently from the others, paid for with my father. I was a boarder who was turned into the maid by his family.

My grandmother slept in a large double bed with a fancy wroth iron headboard and wooden bed frame that held the mattress. Shortly after I arrived in Montego Bay, my father came for a visit from Kingston. That is the only times I ate the same food as everybody and slept next to my grandmother in her bed. I really did not like sleeping in the same bed with her because she smelled funny like an old woman smell. It was not a foul body odor because I would heat water for her and everyone, including myself, to take a bath every day. There was an outside enclosed shower, but there was no hot running water. We had a large wash pan made from zinc which we took to the shower house. We would fill it halfway with cold water from the shower then pour in hot water to take our baths every morning.

My Father's Visit

When my father wrote to say he was coming so soon after my arrival there, I hoped he would place me somewhere else. My grandmother Grammie and Mrs. Queen, her youngest daughter, gave me a warning that things would be worse for me if I did not shut my mouth when my father was visiting. If I said anything Uncle David, my father's older brother, would beat me. My Cousin Trevor was also sleeping on the floor until his mother came for a visit and put a stop to it. My father, on the other hand, only cared that my mother could not find me and believed my grandmother could do nothing wrong.

Mrs. Queen was married with only one child when I arrived in Montego Bay. She did not do any housework at all, that is why I was there. However, she always seemed to be pregnant, but her babies were either still born or they would die shortly after their birth. My grandmother and Mrs. Queen always blamed the death of her children on obeah/witchcraft. Some woman somewhere was always jealous of her and her husband and was trying to destroy her marriage and family. I would wonder to myself, how the obeah/witchcraft of other people can be so deadly against them. Why my grandmother who worked obeah/witchcraft, was not able to see that obeah/witchcraft was being used against her daughter before it was too late? They lived in constant fear and suspicion of everyone and everything all the time. They would always say that they were "bad lucky."

Buried in the Grave

The morning before my father left to return to Kingston, he told me we were going on an outing after I came home from school. I asked if I may know where we were going and he said, No! A car was hired that took me, my father, his mother, Mrs. Queen, and Uncle David on a long drive after dinner. I did not have to cook after school or clean up the kitchen that evening, Trevor did chores when my father was there to hide the fact that I was being mistreated by them. My father told his mother, "This need this to be done before I return to Kingston." I did not know what he meant. I was going to be eight that summer and seven seemed to be the magic age, but for what? We left as it was turning nightfall and drove for a long time. I think we might have gone to another Parish called Trelawny.

The night was pitch black darkness with only the head lights on the car to give some light as we drove away from Montego Bay. There were not many cars on the road because most Jamaicans did not have cars in the 1950's. When you had a car in those days you were a rich big thing, like Mrs. Queens husband, Mr. Sweet Moments. They did not use his car because he did not like obeah.

39

During the car ride, my father asked Mrs. Queen, "What did you tell your husband you were doing tonight?" "I told him we had to see about something in the country with you before you go back to Kingston tomorrow." They seemed to be talking in codes as we drove that evening and I could not make out anything they were saying.

When we were almost there my grandmother took out a can of something from her bag. She opened the can and took out a Vaseline like substance and began to pass it across my eyes and said some words I don't remember hearing before or since. The words had no meaning for me. When we got out of the car, I saw a grave and a small wooden coffin by the grave. I wondered who died, but I was too terrified to ask any questions. Besides I did not want my grandmother and my father to beat me. My father and his mother undressed me in the dark of the night that was lit by a large fire (like a bon fire) out in the open field. They put a white long garment looking like a shroud over me. They then forced me to drink something tasting bitter and awful. I became very tired and sleepy and yet I felt as if I was awake. I had been repeating the 23rd Psalm and the Our Fathers Prayer while we were driving inside because I was so frightened, I did not know what else to do. I still today have no language to explain how it all really felt to be buried while I was alive.

I have since learned that this is a form of Satanic Ritual Abuse, used to re-align a child spiritual compass so that they can be dominated by satanic controls. My father lifted my body and laid me in the coffin that was next to the grave, closed it, and then placed the coffin upside down in the grave. My head went down in the grave first and my feet in the air inside the coffin. I know that I was upside down because I felt my blood rushing to my head, and I lost consciousness. I don't know how long I was in the grave, or when they took me out, or what rituals took place over me while I was in the grave. I did not understand what was wrong with me for days. I was just in a daze not feeling like my old self. Eventually I began to feel somewhat like myself coming back to a different normal. I still looked like myself in the looking glass, but I did not feel the same way as before they buried me in the grave.

When I came to myself my father was already gone back to Kingston without saying goodbye to me. I don't know how long I was in that state of being dazed. I don't know if it was days or weeks. I once asked what happened to me and was told to shut your mouth and stop asking questions you are too inquisitive. I was warned by my grandmother and Mrs. Queen again, that if I told anyone what took place out in the woods that night, bad things would come upon me and my children. During the seven years that I lived with my grandmother, I began to cut and starve myself on purpose. I would get to a place where I felt nothing especially after the burial and cutting myself gave me relief from what I called back then "frozen feelings." However, none of the adults around me seem to comprehend that something was wrong with me being injured on a constant basis. They were all very content to write me off as being a clumsy child. One day I sat among all of them and used one of my father's knives that he used to cut leather and cut a gash on my left thigh about one inch long. When Mrs. Queen watched me doing this, she slapped me hard on my back and called me stupid for cutting myself on purpose. These cutting behaviors continued into my adult life even after I became a born-again believer in 1987.

I have since came to an understanding that in satanic rituals or in any cult environment it is essential that the leaders create an atmosphere for those they wish to dominate and control to buy into their process. Depending on the skills that they have acquired in their demonic partnership with Satan they will employ various combinations of the pain and pleasure principles to motivate those they wish to control and domination. The first line of attack against my human spirit was an overwhelming onslaught of painful experiences employed by the ancient enemy of God against my life. After the individuals spirit is completely broken down, they will gladly buy-in to their domination to decrease their pain unless they have become hardened to pain. In my grandmother's case the pain principle is what she primarily employed in traumatizing my will and break it to her ways.

Pain became a normal part of life to me during those years to the point where any promise of pleasure was so defiled and suspect I would automatically reject them. My grandmother and her daughter Mrs. Queen's offer of a better life if I went along and say the things they wanted me to say always seemed to ring hallow because deep within me I had learned that they would never keep their promise because I only experienced them keeping their promise to give me more pain and never anything that was good. Besides, I looked at both as women who hated me, and I hated them back and I did not want to be anything like them. While I felt powerless as a child concerning the sorrow and grief, they inflicted against me, I felt that I had some measure of internal control to be different from them. That I have come to understand was the sovereign hand of God on my life which blocked my path from total satanic darkness of those adults in my life.

Since I have become a born-again believer, Jesus has been bringing many levels of healing and deliverance into my life to destroy the works of the wicked on. I have renounced, rejected, repudiated, come out of agreements, and alignments with the satanic promises that were spoken by my grandmother and her daughter. All the curses were and are destroyed from me, my sons, and my lineage completely because the Blood of Jesus Christ supersedes all blood oaths and blood covenants, prayed, spoken, and performed against me by the enemy of God. I as a born-again believer have the legal right to nullify all the enemy's demonic devices against me and my family by the power of the Cross and the Blood of Jesus Christ.

CHAPTER THREE

INDOCTRINATION CONTINUES

After being buried my grandmother began to sit me next to her when she gave satanic readings. I was told what she wanted me to say, but I was not able to open my mouth and speak anything she told me to say. I would suddenly go mute when I was told to speak. I could not say anything. Aunt Inez, who was a Seventh Day Adventist, taught me that those types of behavior were of the devil and that people who did such things were evil and would go to hell and burn there when they died, if they did not repent. My grandmother would grab my leg under the table next to her and pinch me so hard I could see fireflies or *pennie wallies*.

Locked in the Chicken Coup

Aunt Inez also taught me scripture that says, you shall have no other gods before me, you shall not bow down to them nor serve them. One time, when I refused to speak lies, my grandmother and Mrs. Queens was so vexed with me that they locked me in the chicken coup for three days and nights without food and they told others not to feed me, either. I was eight years old when this happened. I recited the 23rd Psalm and the Our Father Prayer then and cried a lot. My Aunt Lynette and Mr. Vance, whom you will meet later, would hide and give me food at night after my grandmother went to bed. Aunt Lynette would take the keys from under my grandmother's pillow when she fell asleep because she was a very heavy sleeper. She would open the door of the chicken coop and let me out so I could walk around. I could not walk upright inside the chicken coup because it was not high enough for me to stand up. Aunt Lynette would walk with me to the bathroom because it was dark, and we did not want to awaken anyone by lighting a lamp or using a flashlight. After three days and nights I was officially removed from the chicken coup. Then, I was warned that I would get a worse punishment if I did not say what they told me to say. However, I still was unable to speak the words they wanted me to speak. One day a woman came in and I was unable to say what my grandmother wanted me to say and I began to cry. The woman said to my grandmother that child is not made for this and she left after my grandmother told her the words I could not speak. I was beaten and bruised very hard that evening, but I never had to participate with Grammies' wickedness anymore.

As I listen to her tell these women lies, I would see people who were just confused and losing their way in life. Even as a girl I could not understand how anyone could tell people lies and charge them for it. Or why people believed the lies she told them. Or worse, why people who claimed they believed in God were foolish enough to pay money to hear lies. Since becoming a born-again believer, I repented, renounced, rejected, repudiated, and come out of agreement with all that I was forced to take participate in and witnessed while I was living in Montego Bay with my grandmother. Whenever I would hear her talking with one of her visitors even while sitting next to her, I would begin to recite The Lord's Prayer and the 23rd Psalm in my spirit until the person left. I would also see an angel and a ring of demons on the roof when people were there. Seeing things made me feel like I was a strange child. I saw these things before they buried me. I can see now why God had Aunt Inez teach me The Lord's Prayer and 23rd Psalm and have me memorize them until I could recite them fast without missing a word.

Raped by Cousin Beasley

One Saturday morning when I was about ten years old, a man came to visit Grammie, my grandmother. It seemed that she was expecting him. I was in the kitchen which was separate from the house we lived in cooking breakfast. I was stealing some of the food my father was paying for that I was not allowed to eat. I tried to keep busy but listen to their conversations. I had to be inquisitive in order to find out what was going on around me. Grammie called him Cousin Beasley, they began to speak in very low tones, and I was not able to hear what they were saying. I did hear that he worked at the Stone Quarry and that he had been promoted to foreman. As they talked, I glanced out the window and saw him give her money. He came to the kitchen door as he was leaving and said good morning and good-bye to be at the same time.

My spirit did not take him, the sight of him made me want to vomit. He just seemed slimy, grimy, and nasty all rolled into one. A few weeks went by and Grammie told me one Saturday morning after I came back from the market that she had an errand for me to run. I was to go down to the Stone Quarry where Cousin Beasley worked, and he would give me something for her. What is Cousin Beasley supposed to give me? "Just go and do what I said." She got cross. I asked her if Trevor could go because I had a lot to do on Saturdays. "No, came her reply, I need you to go." "He said to send you." So, to avoid severe punishment, off I went. I walked alone in silence, thinking, wondering what in the world could he have to give her that she could not get for herself. It was not a very long walk and she was able to walk, but I had to go, Trevor could not do the errand. Why me?

When I got to the Stone Quarry, I saw a young girl about my age coming out a small side room, crying. I did not know her, but she was crying, and I wondered why. I asked the gate man for Mr. Beasley. He let me in through the gate and closed it behind me then began to laugh. When I saw Cousin Beasley coming out of the same room as the crying girl I began to turn and run. He caught me by the hem of my dress before I could squeeze through the opening in the gate. The gate man began to laugh again, and I wished I could throw a rock stone at him for laughing at me. Cousin Beasley dragged me inside a small, dingy, smelly, room with a small cot that had two wooden staves on each side and two legs crossed at each end. It was covered with a dirty nasty piece of canvas.

Cousin Beasley roughly pushed me into one of the corners opposite the cot, put his hand over my mouth and he raped me. I felt sick and my head began to spin. I felt like my bowels were going to explode. I bit his hand because he was hurting me. He gave me a back handed slap across my face with the hand that was over my mouth and told me "never do that again." I felt blood running from the corner of my mouth. I began to vomit which began to run through his hand, but he did not stop or move his hand from my mouth. When he was finished, he gave me five shillings for my grandmother the equivalent of $5.00 at the time. He warned me to shut my mouth. "Grammie, your grandmother knew what I would do to you for her to get my money." He then told me "get out of my room, I will see you again in two weeks." He rapes me and then has the cheek to be disgusted and show contempt against me. That piece of dung, that slime bucket, that venomous predatory victimizer that was fronting as a man.

I left crying just like the girl before me. I stopped and vomited some more on the way home. When I got to the house, I gave the five shillings to Grammie, she was happy. I thought to myself, my grandmother is selling her soul and me for money. The corner of my mouth was still bleeding slightly, but she did not ask me why I was bleeding or what happened. I was hurting very badly, not walking properly for the pain of being raped, and I also felt sore for days. I decided that day that I really hated my father for sending me to live with his mother. I also decided that day, I hated my grandmother. I knew the first chance got to leave Montego Bay I would take it and never look back.

Back to Beasley

I was in a lot of torment about the fact that I would have to go back to see Cousin Beasley and be raped again. The closer the time came towards two weeks, the more I began to agonize about going back there. I vowed I would not go. I would take the beatings that I knew would be coming because I refused to do what she said. I shared my secret with my two friends, and we came up with a plan. I would leave the yard to go and walk close the Stone Quarry, wait for some time. Then go back home and tell Grammie that Cousin Beasley was not there. So that is what I did. I could see when I came into the yard and told my grandmother he was not there that she did not believe me. However, she said nothing. That Saturday night we were frying fish, dumplings, yellow and green plantains, and drinking lemonade and hot tea. I knew that the issue of Cousin Beasley would be coming up when they thought I least expected it. When all the eating and telling jokes were over and I was on my way into the kitchen to clean up, Uncle David said, "What a shame that Cousin Beasley was not there today." I looked at him very seriously. I did not know what to say. So, I said nothing, and the matter was dropped.

Two weeks later on a Saturday morning I was sent to see Cousin Beasley again. Grammie, said as I was leaving the yard, "I know Cousin Beasley will be there today." I began crying as soon as I left the yard. On my way there I saw Aunt Lynette who wanted to know what was wrong that I was crying. I told her what Cousin Beasley had done to me the first time that I went there before he gave me money for Grammie. That the next time I did not go and I had to lie. She told me that Cousin Beasley had done the same thing to her when she was a girl about my age.

She also told me her mother and my grandmother, did not send Mrs. Queen to Cousin Beasley. She gave me five shillings to give to Grammie each time that I had to go. Aunt Lynette and I developed a routine, where she would leave out of the yard first. I would leave when it was time for me to go to Cousin Beasley and we would meet up talk for the time frame and I would return home with five shillings for my grandmother. This was a great sacrifice for Aunt Lynette because she worked only a few days out of each week cleaning house, ironing, or washing for other people. She did not get paid very much. Her sacrifice kept me from being raped over-and-over-again the way that she was. I am grateful that I did not have to go back to Cousin Beasley and be raped repeatedly.

Hiding under the Cellar

One Sunday evening after dinner however, Cousin Beasley came into the yard and he was very cross. When I saw him I almost fainted? He addressed my grandmother very harshly wanting to know why I was not being sent to see him every other Saturday as they had arranged. I ran and hid myself deep under the cellar of the house behind Mr. Vance's room. Grammie would not be able to come and get me for my beating after he left. She let it go and I slept under the cellar that night, I was afraid of the rats, but I did not want to be beaten so I prayed my prayers. Grammie sent Trevor to get Uncle David who was the cruelest beater man you ever want to meet. They found a letter that a boy in school had written to me which was hidden under the floorboard of the house. I had not done anything with the boy, but I was beaten because a boy in my class wrote me a love letter. Uncle David was inside the house waiting until I came home from school that evening. He hid behind the wardrobe and as soon as my uniform was off, he came out from where he and began to beat with twisted electric wires when I was only in my underwear.

Uncle David did not come that night or the next day, so I had to come out and do my chores to keep from making things worse for myself. Mrs. Queen and my grandmother wanted to know where I had stolen five shillings every two weeks since I was not getting it from Cousin Beasley. I told them I borrowed it from my friends, but Aunt Lynette chimed in and told them she was giving me the money so that Beasley would not spoil Vivienne anymore the way that he had spoiled me. She was forced by her mother Grammie to go to Beasley for many years. She also asked my grandmother, "Why did you send me to that Beasley when you knew what he would do to me?" "Why is it that your other daughters Mrs. Queen and Verdi never had to go?" "What made Mrs. Queen and Verdi better than me or Vivienne?" "Vivienne is your grandchild!" I knew as a child that while Aunt Lynette was very sweet and quiet, she was angry, but I never knew why until that day. Whenever, I would ask her why she was so vexed, she would say "who told you that I am vexed?" "You look vexed all the time auntie," I would say to her, but the subject was always dropped.

When Uncle David came into the yard on the third day, I knew that he would come under the cellar to get me. I also knew he was going to beat me to death for lying to his mother. It would not matter to him that I lied to keep from being raped by Cousin Beasley. However, when he got there, I heard him tell my grandmother that there was some bad news. The Stone Quarry foreman, Cousin Beasley was found dead in his room the night before and the gate man was now promoted to his position. I only felt relief. I did not really care anymore if Uncle David beat me, so I came out. I was free from being raped by that Beasley. I did not attend his funeral, I got sick that morning. I began to vomit at the thought of seeing him in the casket or anywhere else for that matter. Neither did Aunt Lynette, we stayed home and cooked fried fish and bammy, made lemonade for them to eat after the funeral. I saw everyone after they came back to our yard for dinner following the funeral. Some relatives were saying what a shame that he was dead, and no one know who strangled him. He was a very strong man so it would have taken someone stronger than him to strangle him.

During those years I kept trying to find my mother. I finally found her through Aunt Inez and wrote to her asking if I could come live with her because of the bad treatment that I was getting from my father's family. My mother wrote back to say I was better off where I was because her husband was a violent man who would beat her badly. This was very disappointing news to hear. I felt that there was no refuge for me. I was trapped with Grammie and her daughter Mrs. Queen doing whatever they wanted to do to me because my father only cared I was not with my mother.

Mr. Sweet Moments

When I lived with my father, I had a few chores, and my father had a woman who would come and clean our apartment. When I went to live with my grandmother Grammie, I had the responsibility to do all of the marketing and a lot of the cooking and ironing on Friday afternoons instead of being in school. In the beginning I did not know how to cook, being just seven years old when I arrived there. My aunt's husband was called Mr. Sweet Moments. I never found out why everyone called him that or some would call him Moments. I also never learned what his real first name was. He refused to eat any leftovers. All of his meals were to be bought daily from the market and cooked fresh. I was put in charge of going to the market daily to purchase the days meals. His dinner must be hot and on the dinner table with steam coming off the serving dishes when he came home from the mechanic shop. He owned his mechanic shop with apprentices and the contract to repair the police department cars in Montego Bay. He is what we would call-well to do in those days. Well to do was what is considered upper middle class. His argument was that he provided well so Mrs. Queen did not have go out and work. He, therefore, expected that she would go to the market daily and be the wife that prepared his meals the way that he wanted them since she did not have to go out and work or do any of the housework.

My trips to the Meat Market was often time very adventurous to say the least because as a small girl, I was competing with adult women in a culture where children were to be seen and not heard. It was very difficult to get the attention of the butchers in order to get the cut of meat that I was told to buy each day. Some of the women were wives, mothers and others were maids who were doing the marketing for their employers. Some days, I would stand there, and it was as if my presence was not seen and my voice was not heard no matter how loudly I tried to articulate what it was that I was there to buy. Needless-to-say, some days I did not get the cut of meat they wanted and some days I got nothing at all to buy because they would sell out of meat or chicken.

Sometimes I would go and buy fish down by the Warf, but they only wanted fish on Fridays or sometimes on Saturdays. Each day there was a specific menu that was to be prepared. One day while I was trying to buy meat for soup and was not being heard I just broke down and began to cry because the day before

I was not only beaten, but I went without food all day for not bringing home Stew Beef, Salt Beef and Red Peas to make Stew Peas and Rice for the evening meal.

God's Hand of Intervention

One of the women who seemed to have some influence with the butcher, asked him to serve me two pounds of soup meat before he made her order ready for her. With the two pounds of soup meat, I also purchased quarter pound of Salt Beef because that is how Mrs. Queens' husband liked his soup and Stew Peas to be made. I was so grateful to that lady that I offered to help her carry her bankra load to the bus that she was taking back home. I would make sure to look for her each time I went to the market. When she was there, I could get what I was sent to buy. It turned out that she had her own shop in Mt. Salem, a town outside of Montego Bay, and would come and purchase meat to sell in her shop.

Market Days

Going to the market was the task for a woman, not a young girl. I was awakened before daybreak each morning and I would walk in the darkness to the market. The streetlights were few and far between, so I would walk in the middle of the road because I was so afraid that I would be grabbed or hurt by someone. I carried a basket/bankra to bring the day's meats and ground provisions home. I was required to purchase foods based on the menu that Mr. Sweet Moments wanted. This daily marketing chore was to be done by Mrs. Queen his wife a woman who would have been respected at marketplace because of her husband's status in the community.

Whenever I did not get the meat, they wanted I learned to buy fish, tripe, or whatever else I could buy. I would be beaten often for not bringing home from the market what was wanted because they would be sold out by the time, they came around to the little gal. One morning when I was sick from bleeding, vomiting, with headaches from having my period, the meal that Mr. Sweet Moments wanted to have that evening was not purchased because by the time Mrs. Queen got up, had her bath, got dressed and went to the market they were sold out of everything.

Mrs. Queens Marketing Experience

She purchased Ackee which is an edible fruit that was brought to Jamaica from West Africa in the 18th century. Ackee and salted Cod Fish with ground provisions for dinner which my grandmother cooked. Ground provisions are white sweet potatoes, yellow yams, green bananas, and cornmeal dumplings. Now, any Jamaican will tell you that this is a fine meal, but he had a menu and she was expected to cook based on what he wanted to eat each day and was able to provide for his family. When Mr. Sweet Moments came home the table was set, and their family sat down to eat. When Mr. Sweet Moments opened the serving dishes and saw that he was being fed Ackee and salted Cod Fish with ground provisions he became enraged. This is Wednesday and I came home ready to eat a hot plate of Stew Peas with Salt Beef, and Rice for dinner which I told you this morning. Mrs. Queen began to try and explain that Vivienne was sick this morning and could not go to the market. This is what I was able to get because I was late getting to the market. Tomorrow, Vivienne will get there early and I will have it for you on the table nice and hot when you come home. "Vivienne, who is Vivienne? You are married to me. Vivienne is a little gal; you are my wife. Don't tell me about Vivienne."

The next thing I heard was Mrs. Queen screaming. Moments! You can't throw away all this food as he grabbed all four corners of the tablecloth, napkins, plates, serving dishes, all the food, serving utensils and threw them out of their dining room window. He then began to curse up a blue, yellow purple streak of Jamaican cuss words stringing them together that I will NOT repeat. I was sipping on a hot cup of tea when, to my horror, the food along with all the dishes came flying out the dining room window. He left the house in his car speeding and cussing as he went. I can still see everything flying out the window to this day. All the food and dishes landed in the entrance of Mr. Vance's' room. Mr. Vance had to sweep up all the broken pieces of dishes with the food when he got home from the field that evening.

I sat there and smirked to myself at the irony of Useless Mrs. Queen as an adult not being able to get what she wanted to purchase for dinner at the market. Yet, I as a girl would be beaten and sometimes not fed and berated and made to feel like a failure for what she as an adult could not accomplish. I did not feel a bit sorry for her. She got her beating in a different way than I would have gotten mine. My grandmother saw the smirk on my face and told me to straighten up my face, what is there to laugh about. Yes Grammie, I said as I went to lay under her bed and laughed at her and her daughter.

Cooking and Eating Crabs

One of the only times that I could get out of the chores of going to the market daily was during the crabbing season each year or serious illness. Crabbing season was a special time when they would go crabbing in specific places which I was not allowed to tag along because women might scare the crabs off. This is something men say when they want to bond alone without women, it's like football. The men would return with burlap bags full of crabs that were cooked at night, and the neighbors were invited to come and eat crabs with us. The men would drink White Rum, Red Stripe Beer, play dominos, Ludy a board game played with dice, cards, and talk very loudly as if they were all deaf, slapping the game boards with their hands when their team made a better play than the other team. The women would drink Rum Punch, hot tea, lemonade, Ginger Beer. Ginger Beer it is like root Beer. It is grated or ground ginger and mixed with boiling water. Rice grains would be placed in the hot liquid which is covered and left to ferment overnight. The liquid is then strained through a clean cloth and the liquid sweetened with brown sugar or molasses. I never saw the women drinking liquor because that was in poor taste for females in Jamaica of that era. Whenever a woman drank a beer, she was considered the worst sort of woman who was not fit for marriage to a decent Jamaican man.

There would be music playing but no one would dance. They would only listen and sing along to the beat and rhythm of the Jamaican music. While at home the only music I heard was Jamaican music on Saturday mornings. On Sunday morning gospel hymns would be played on the radio. It was only at the Library in town that I would hear what I was told was classical music being played by a live band. The men talked politics with great intelligence and clarity, considering that most of them were functionally literate but not formerly educated. It is somewhat amazing to me today their levels of intelligence and clarity about the political matters of Jamaica. While the men talked politics, the women talked about their family bragging on their husbands and children's scholastic achievements.

Late for School

I was usually late for school every day because ALL my chores had to be completed before I left for school. I had to make all the beds, dust all their furniture, and clean and shine all the floors with Bees Wax and a Coconut Brush on my knees with my hands. One morning Mrs. Queen got angry because I was crying while I was shining the floor and took a bucket of water and poured it all over the floor that I was almost finish shining. I had to start all over and by the time I got to school it was almost lunch time. Now schools in Jamaica did not take too kindly to children being late, so we would be punished for lateness and we had to make up all the work that was missed. I joined the track team and played volleyball, at Montego Bay Senior School. I had to give up some other freedom in order to participate in those sports. To be placed in high school I had to take the Common Entrance Exam. So, we were given extra lessons that prepared us to take the exams. I would study late into the nights by a kerosene lamp to try and catch up because I was kept out of school on Mrs. Queens's whims sometimes. The level of your score on the Common Entrance Exams determined what high school you would be attending. Those children who could not afford prep schools were able to attend free public schools which do a good job.

Mr. Sweet Moments in Hiding

Mr. Sweet Moments got in some trouble shortly after Cousin Beasley funeral. Before he went away to England, he went into hiding because his life was in danger. I was never able to find out everything, but according to the gossip, he was committing adultery with the wife of the Chief of Police. He went into hiding in the Parish of St Catherine where we had family. His and Mrs. Queen's names were taken off the list of other social gatherings and they were no longer welcomed at the Annual Policeman's Ball. According to the gossip, their adulterous relationship had been going on for years and Mrs. Queen did not know about it. Mrs. Queen and the chief's wife were friends and they talked with each other about their husbands all the time when the chief's wife would visit with her at the house. Yet, she was clueless that one of her good friends was betraying her with her husband. Again, I began to wonder how Grammie who was working obeah/witchcraft did not see what was happening. I wondered how that information escaped them when it came to Mr. Sweet Moments. With all of their probing suspicions they missed the most important information that concerned them the most. What was the point of their obeah/witchcraft, I would think as a girl, when it could not protect them? Yet, I did not know who could!

Mrs. Queen's Surprise Visitor

We had a surprise visitor come to our gate one evening. She stood with her hands her hips and cursed Mrs. Queen out telling her that she was one going to England as the wife of Mr. Moments. The entire yard looked on in delight, amazement, anger, and wonder as Mrs. Queen stood there listened carefully, but said nothing. Some of the women in the yard were offering to hold her so that Mrs. Queen could beat her in her face, but she said no, leave her alone. "But she is stealing away your husband man! Let us beat her for you, No!" Although Mrs. Queen said no to everybody in the yard about beating the girl, I think the girl got a beating from her and Uncle David at another time.

After the woman left that night, I heard Mrs. Queen crying buckets of tears. Although she was not my favorite aunt because of how mean she was to me, I felt badly for her. Mrs. Queen treated everybody as if they were simply beneath her. We only existed to serve her every whim. That same night she sent my cousin Trevor to get Uncle David, but I did not hear all their conversation when he came. As he was leaving the yard, he promised that he would take care of all the arrangements by morning. Everything will be in order, depend on it said Uncle David. Very early the next morning Mrs. Queen and both of her children were in a car that came to the house to take them from Montego Bay to Kingston.

The night before my grandmother told me to hurry and pack Mrs. Queen's and the children's suitcase while the conversation took place between her and Uncle David. During the night she continued to search and gather various documents, including the marriage certificate, birth certificates, and baptismal certificates for the children with pictures of her and Mr. Sweet Moments at their wedding when she was pregnant with their first child Roland. Mrs. Queen had pictures of her, Mr. Sweet Moments and the children taken before he sailed for England. All this documentation was to prove that they were married and had two children. In addition, while she was waiting for him to send for them, she got all their passports ready. She took all of this to the British Embassy in Kingston to inform them that the woman who claimed to be married to her husband was an imposter.

Mrs. Queen's Gracious Intrigue

While she was in Kingston for three weeks, she stayed with my grandmother's sister, Aunt Brownie. Before she left for Kingston, she asks some of the neighbors who were watching the spectacle of her shame and disgrace to write letters stating what the girl said to her about her husband. I learned that a telegram was sent to Great Aunt Brownie to expect Mrs. Queen and the two children for as long as her business would take in Kingston. The money that my father sent to take care of me went to fund that cause. When Mrs. Queen came home from Kingston, she had visas for herself, and her two children to leave from Jamaica to England in twenty-one days. She then went to her father who booked the passage for her and the two children to London

England. Mr. Joseph her father was cross and cussing Moments for his behaviors. He helped to fund Mr. Moments' in getting his mechanic business started and introduced him to the Chief of Police. He was also upset that he was taking his youngest daughter and her children away from him. Mrs. Queen prevailed on him to let her go because "Moments is my husband; I love him, and I don't want to lose my family to that woman."

No one except for her and my grandmother knew all the details; the children were not told that they were leaving for England until just before. She also did not write to Mr. Sweet Moments telling him that she would be coming to England so that he could expect them in London rather than his concubine. She was told by the British Embassy that they would handle all of the details of notifying him. She was also informed by the Embassy that if her husband refused to accept them in London, she should contact them, and they would take the matter from there. Refusing to accept his wife and children in England would most likely have gotten him deported back to Jamaica. No Jamaican or anyone from another country wants to be deported back to their country. It's just too shaming. Besides there is always a suspicion that you did something wrong to get yourself kicked out of the foreign country if you return home before retirement.

In Mr. Sweet Moments case, there was the death threat against life in Jamaica. Whatever his plans were, his behaviors had changed those plans for him. I heard that when he to meet the concubine and saw his wife and children he was shocked beyond belief. They did go home to together and had two more children in England. While the marriage continued to be a rocky because of her lack of housekeeping skills, and his womanizing, they stayed together for a while. I met her some years ago here in America and she said that he left her for yet another woman. She got financial support and refused to divorce him.

My Aunt Lynette

Looking back, I understand now that my Aunt Lynette was a deeply traumatized woman. Yet the sweetest most lovable human being I have ever had the pleasure of knowing and being around. While Mrs. Queen was a lazy self-centered spoiled brat, Aunt Lynette was the total opposite. Within her family system she was considered dumb or stupid. In those days Jamaican families did not like it when they had a child that was different or considered funny because they lacked potential for academic achievement whatever the reason. Aunt Lynette was the third child for my grandmother Grammie and Mr. Joseph's. On the day of Cousin Beasley's funeral, she told me that Grammie sent her to Cousin Beasley when she was almost ten. My Aunt Lynette broke down sobbing when she told me her story of how he raped her repeatedly. I was holding and rocking her saying the Our Father Prayer and the 23rd Psalm over her as she cried in my arms when I almost eleven.

Aunt Lynette was simply not capable of hate, or any type of guile, it was she who would come to my defense and rescue me because she simply could not stand to see me being hurt. She would hold me and rock me kissing me on my head and on my cheek whenever I was beaten by other family members. Sometimes she would put coconut oil on my bruises and wounds, with warm cloths to help soothe my pain. She never had much in the way of possessions or money to give to any of her nieces or nephews, but what money she had she gave to us with a love that did not exist in any other members of my father's family. When she got married, I was living with my mother in Kingston. Aunt Lynette always talk about getting married and she eventually became Mrs. Brown. They had one son whom she named Liston Joseph Brown. Her son Liston did not survive beyond a few months and she died less than a year after his death. I was told that her husband Mr. Brown died shortly after her and they were both buried by the lodges that she belonged to. She paid monthly dues that was recorded in a book which she kept close watch over. I really do not know much about this lodge. I believe it was some aspect of a Freemasonry Lodge for women in Jamaica. She would tell us when she got back from the monthly meetings or any of their functions that she was not allowed to tell us anything about it and she never did. Aunt Lynette was loyal to her lodge the way that some people are loyal to their churches or social Clubs.

Mr. Vance

There were a few people in my life that made life more bearable because they would show me loving kindness. Mr. Vance was a very tall, high yellow or Jamaican white as they were sometimes called in those days was a tenant of ours. He lived under the high cellar of the house given to Mrs. Queen by her father not to own but to live in. He did not pay rent because he was a relative of her husband. Both Mr. Sweet Moments and Mr. Vance were the outside sons of married men from the same wealthy family. These married men did not own up to either of their sons and made no provisions for them to be educated or learn a trade.

They were in their teens when each of their mother's got married. Their mother's new husbands sent them out on their own. Mr. Vance would tell the story that his stepfather told him, he did not want to look in my father's face each time he came into his own house. Mr. Vance said that his mother was a nursemaid for a wealthy family when she was only sixteen. He said his father who was the master of the house raped his mother. However, when his wife found out that she had been raped she accused her seducing her husband and threw her out that same day. She later learned that she was pregnant with him. Mr. Vance told us he became a Seventh Day Adventist because his mother and all his family were. He was a boy of fourteen when his stepfather sent him out on his own. He became a day laborer working the field which he did until he died. He said that he would meet his mother in the market after he left home and she would give him food for the week asking him not to let it get back to her husband that she was providing food for him.

Mr. Vance would always tell me that God was going to change my life someday. He used to read the Bible to me and my cousins on Sabbath Evenings which were Friday evenings after sundown. Although he was married, his wife would only come and visit him every other week on payday. She was the opposite of Mr. Vance, who was friendly and kind. I never saw him get vexed or heard him raise his voice to anyone in a cross word. On the other hand, Mrs. Vance was always cross. Nothing seemed to be able to make her smile. He once said: "My wife cannot be pleased no matter what I do." They had a daughter who Mr. Vance was putting through private school.

I remember being very jealous of her because I had a half scholarship a year earlier and my grandmother went with me for an interview at Mt. Alvernia High School and I was accepted. She later said my father would not be wasting his money to send me to high school because all I was going to do is get pregnant and have children without a husband. I was crushed. Those words intensified my hatred for my grandmother. I badly wanted an education and hoped that studying in high school might give me a bit of status and a chance to change my life in the future. Mr. Vance was very proud of his only daughter and would tell us and that it was worth it for him to be away from his wife so that he could provide her with an education. I wished I had a father that would provide for my education without being influenced by my grandmother.

In Jamaica there are three major core values. Loving, serving God, and your country, loving your family, and becoming educated to advance your future. All our other values are attached to these. In Jamaica when a woman is educated, she has more status and choices available to her about who she marries and the outcomes of her life. A parent's first question to their friends is where they attend high school. I badly wanted to achieve the status of being an educated Jamaican woman. I felt a deep sense of shame about not going to high school and wanted to matter to myself. When my father married Elsa, my name was placed on his list of candidates for sponsorship to America. Shortly after Mrs. Queen left for England with her children, I received a letter from my father stating that my name was called, and I needed to go to Kingston to begin my process to come to America. He and Elsa decided to move away from my grandmother in Montego Bay to live in Kingston. I would be staying with Aunt Rona, Elsa's sister in Vineyard Town, Kingston.

CHAPTER FOUR

BACK IN KINGSTON

I cannot remember what mode of transportation took me to Vineyard Town in Kingston. The purpose of going back to Kingston was to prepare for going to the United States. This was in 1964, but by the time the paperwork process was completed for me to be granted a visa it was 1966. In Vineyard Town I was given a room to sleep in which was the smallest room in the back of the house, but I was not sleeping on the floor and I had my own room it was great to have privacy. Moving to begin the paperwork process with the American Embassy meant that I was no longer attending senior school. Besides me, there were three other teenage girls in the home of the Sanford's. As soon as I arrived in Vineyard Town, I was accompanied by Aunt Rona's husband, Uncle Kirc, to the American Embassy for a scheduled appointment.

I helped with the chores and I could eat the same food with the family at the dining table at Aunt Rona's. One of the things I had in common with the three other girls is, we were all abandoned by our mothers. While the other girls went to school, I was at home and feeling angry and resentful that I had to leave senior school and would not be graduating with my peers that year. I was aware that I would have opportunities in America, yet not attending school in Jamaica was a sore point in my life. I asked Aunt Rona one evening if I could be registered to attend a free high school while I was waiting for my visa. If I took and passed the entrance exam, then I would only need uniforms, money for books, lunch and daily travel expenses.

She told me she would write and ask my father if that was possible. Aunt Rona later told me that it was not a good idea for me to go to high school because I had missed too much schooling, I would not be able to keep up and graduate. She felt that I was too far gone to be properly educated so I should take up a trade like hairdressing. Being a hairdresser is a great trade, except I had no interest in becoming proficient at doing hair for the rest of my life. I wanted to be educated. My father was given this same information and he simply accepted it about me. He never questioned whether I could make up my educational losses with extra lessons. I was greatly disappointed and angry because the female adults in my life kept deciding on my future and my father would roll over and say yes. He never put up any defense for me on the issue of my education or anything else. The only female in my life that he loved fighting against concerning me was my mother. Aunt Rona was a Psychiatric Head Nurse at the Island's psychiatric hospital, Bellevue.

I got into an angry argument with one of the other girls one evening, when she said, "No man will want you, because you're not being educated like us." When she heard that her stepdaughters were plotting to beat me up, she became concerned that it would be two against one. However, I sensed she felt I was not a good fit for her family dynamics at the time. When it became clear that my documentation would be a lengthy process, she wanted to settle me elsewhere. The other girls were jealous because I was going to America as soon as all my paperwork was completed. One another incident almost lead to a fight on the verandah with one of her stepdaughter's over the same issue but her mother stepped in and broke us up before we came to blows.

Finding My Mother

I kept the letter I received from my mother while I lived in Montego Bay. I asked Uncle Kirc if he could help me find my mother on one of our trips to the American Embassy. I told him I had a letter from her, when she lived on Woodpecker Avenue in Coburn Gardens. When we got to the American Embassy that day, we were told that until I found my mother the process for my visa could not go any further. Uncle Kirc asked "Why?" He was told my mother had to sign a Declaration of Independence releasing me to go to my father because I was under the age of consent. I gave him the letter I kept from her and he used his connection as a police officer to try and find her. However, after several weeks he was still unable to find her, but he located her sister Inez.

Aunt Rona and I went to Aunt Inez's home one Sunday morning to see if she had any information on locating my mother. She was not home, but her son Stephen knew where my mother was and took us to see her. Meeting face-to-face with my mother for the first time since I was seven years old was a bitter-sweet experience. I was now fourteen. She looked the same, but different at the same time. My cousin greeted my mother and she looked at me and asked him. "Who is this lady pointing to me?" I was crushed that she did not appear to recognize me. Aunt Ruth, this is Vivienne, your daughter. "Oh, you are Vivienne." Aunt Rona was standing there looking at us and I wondered what she was thinking about me meeting with my mother for the first time in over seven years. Later that day when I saw my Aunt Inez, she instantly knew me and hugged me. My mother never hugged me. My mother seemed very cold and distant even though she smiled.

Living with My Mother's Anger

I told my mother that I needed a form called Declaration Independence signed by her so that my father could sponsor me to America. My mother said, "after all his fighting me to take you from me, now he needs my permission to have you in America." It was there that I introduced Aunt Rona to my mother. Aunt Rona and my mother walked away from us and talked a while. I stood next to my cousin Stephen and watched their body language wondering what would happen. I pondered, would I be staying at Aunt Rona's or would my mother still want me? When the conversation was over, I went back with Aunt Rona and gathered my few belongings that night. The following day Aunt Rona took me to live with my mother. I still had my Delcemina Grip. While it was quite worn, I still had it. She was living in a room that she was renting with one of my younger brother Samuel who I had never met before. It took a longtime and a lot of hard work to forgive her for not recognizing who I was when she first saw me. While it had been over seven years, I still remembered her look. So how could she not remember me, her child?

My mother would vent her frustrations over her life when she talked about her past with me. In all her tirades about the pain of my father's brutishness towards her, blinded her to the impact of her rage against him on me. The painful issues of her own life left her incapable of comprehending the signs of his brutishness and cruelties towards me as well. My father's brutishness also numbed her to the emotional needs of the daughter she abandoned.

She had gotten married and opened a grocery store with her husband, they saved up to purchase a house in Jamaica. Through a crocked housing scheme, she lost her house after the death of her husband. The house was in his name and the name of housing agents. Mr. Byron could not read but my mother could, however, he wanted to do business without her. In the pride and shame over his illiteracy, he cheated his children and left his wife destitute of what they had worked so hard to achieve.

When I first came to live with my mother she was working and I had the responsibility to keep the room clean, cook, and take care of one of my brothers. He was the first child of her marriage followed by my younger brother Paul. Her older son in the marriage was considered the brilliant one in the family. The pride of my mother's heart, for whatever he told her I did wrong, she believed him, and I was in trouble. My mother finally did sign my Declaration of Independence but the paperwork process for my visa went on a stand still. I was hoping that going back to my mother would be a place of acceptance; however, I felt I was there because she needed me and not because she wanted me. She equated my five feet, seven-inch stature as a sign that I was an adult woman. However, on the inside I was still the seven-year-old girl, she left on the steps of my father's apartment, with a promise to return for me. While it was not her fault, I was sent away I felt trapped in the traumatic time bonds of abandonment by both of my parents.

I Wanted to Return to School

I desperately wanted to return to some type of education, so she sent me learn how to become a dressmaker. Learning sewing was something to do and I made the best of it while still having a deep longing within me to be educated rather than learning a trade. Being educated was a deep need for me, maybe because my father's family, while they did all they could to keep me from going to school, would constantly call me a dunce. (A dunce is a person who is dull witted, stupid, or an ignorant person; a dolt). Shortly after I came to live with her and was going to sewing, she had a nervous breakdown. Well the nervous breakdown was already in progress before I entered back into her life. I remembered being in the doctor's office and my mother was being told by the doctor "you are having a nervous breakdown and would need to stop working for a while." I wondered to myself: how in the world can nerves breakdown! I did not understand the term nervous breakdown. I had to go to work in order for us to survive financially. One of the sisters in my mother's church got me a job working with her.

Her employer was an importer-exporter of rare postage stamps. I had the responsibility to put the stamps in deep pans of water and carefully remove each stamp from the piece of envelope it was attached to without damaging the points. I went back to daydreaming about being a writer, but still never shared it with anyone. After I came home from work, I cooked, and did the household chores because, my mother could not. In the middle of all this my sister Sharon who I did not known ran away from the cruel treatment of where she was staying and came to live with my mother. I had another sibling to care for because she was thirteen and I was almost sixteen by then. I was fired one morning during my workday when I fainted at work.

Locked out by My Mother

The reason that we were locked out of the house is because one of my younger brothers told my mother, "Vivienne did not feed me all day today." He was only about six, but he began to cry as soon as she came home, she became upset. When she asked him what was wrong, he told her his tearful story of not being fed. We all had a cup of bush/herbal tea that morning without sugar, but nothing else was available to eat. I was waiting for her to come home so that we could all eat. At the time she returned to work as a domestic worker she was not fully recovered from her nervous breakdown. I was the mother to her children while she worked away from home and came home once each week. She cooked from what she brought home, fed herself and her son, but did not offer me or my sister any of the food. She screamed at us and told me I was wicked for not feeding her son. She never bothered to inquire if any of her other children ate all that day.

If my mother inquired, she would have learned, none of her children ate because we had no food. Nothing! No bread, not even crackers, no flour, and no cornmeal available. She was working but it did not pay her very well so we would run out of food no matter how much I tried to stretch what she provided there was never enough for us to eat. Since she was cursing us out, we went outside and stayed away from her. When my sister and I attempted to walk up the steps to go into the room to go to sleep that night, she pushed us back, slammed and locked the door. We spent the night sleeping on the benches of a day school that consisted of one enclosed wall. So, we were in an open space sleeping on the benches. I felt such a strong surge of rage and bitterness towards her that night.

I Found Another Job

The following morning, I borrowed money from a neighbor and bought a newspaper to look for work. I found a job as a nursemaid taking care of a little girl. A nursemaid meant I was caring for the couple's child as well and doing all of the housework. This lasted less than a week. A few days after I began working there, the wife of the house went away to the country taking her daughter with her to see about her sick mother. The wife told me I could sleep in the house in her spare bedroom while she was gone. It would only have been me and her husband alone in her house. I told her I would prefer to sleep in my room in the back of the house. I felt it would be safer because I did not like the way that her husband looked at me when I was serving them dinner. The look on his face towards me was the same look I saw on Cousin Beasley's face before my grandmother sent me to see him. Her husband's looking at me made me afraid of being raped by him.

The Fear of Being Raped

I locked and bolted my room door and went to bed early that night after she left. During the night I heard a loud banging to open the door. It was the woman's husband demanding that I open my door. "Let me in, I am lonely for wife." I was glad I did not agree to sleep in their spare bedroom. I was terrified and refused to open the door. When I threatened to tell his wife that he was asking to come to my room, he told me, "My wife knows that I do this." If you tell her you are the one who will be in trouble with her." I refused to let him into my room and he finally left, but not before making a loud commotion. The following morning was Wednesday, I started this job on Sunday. I did not sleep that night I stayed awake crying and praying. I waited in my room until I heard his car drive away the next morning, then took my few belongings and ran away, I never went back for my three day's pay.

Working as a Nanny

I did not tell my mother what happened, but I shared it with my sister and told her I was not going back there. Wednesday night at youth meeting, one of the sisters at church told me about a position with the family she worked for as a housekeeper. They were looking for a Nanny to care their son and it was a live-in position. I was hired on the spot after the interview. This live-in Nanny situation was perfect because my mother and I were not getting along. I could go home every weekend, but I opted to go home every other week for one afternoon and one Sunday each month. While I was living with my mother it was mandatory that I attend church. The church that my mother attended were hardline Pentecostals. No perming or hot pressing of my hair, no makeup, no pants. These rules were outward signs of holiness, but nothing could have been further from the truth. If we visited a sister church without permission on a night, we did not have church we had to go to the front and repent to the leaders, not to God. We were not allowed to do much of anything. I hated church and I hated my mother for wanting me to serve her God. At the time I saw the God my mother served as abandoning as her and my father were. In time she recovered from her nervous breakdown and returned to a better paying job. Life had taken its toll on my mother and her misery over her past with failed relationships was taking its toll on me. I wanted out of the situation because I had no way to reconcile any of it. My father and her husband were brutish men. To her, all men were brutish. I believed there was some truth to her statement. Some men and women were and are brutish, but not all.

I remember thinking to myself, I am only sixteen years old. Why are all these adults expecting me to be an adult when I am just a girl? Looking back, I lost my entire childhood. Yet, I was the only one who seemed to care and feel that this was not right or good for me. I was made fun of for lamenting that I was never allowed to be a child by the adults in my life. Or that my father used me for his twisted satisfaction and stole my innocence before I knew myself or had the capacity to make the choice to give myself to anyone. I was told, don't ever say that! People will say it is your fault that your father raped you. Whenever, I made any attempts to talk about how much I wanted my life to matter I was scolded and told to just let the past go! How? The adults that I grew up around never let anything go. They said they did, but as they spoke about their past, I would watch their body language and their faces contorting in pain. These behaviors confused me as a girl growing up it left me wondering what was real in interpersonal relationships.

It has since become my observation of human beings that most of us do not forget the past or find closure. What most of us frail humans beings do, is bury our pain alive. I know today that pain that is buried alive, stays alive, and comes alive each time that someone bumps our live pain. Buried pain stays alive in our subconscious and interferes with our future until we heal the traumas. After about six months working as a Nanny, my visa was granted, and I left and came to America.

Chapter Five

America

After my visa was granted for America, I was excited and looking forward to a change with better days ahead. I had met Elsa just before she married my father and she was kind to me. Although I was in Kingston, I was not allowed to attend their wedding because I was required to babysit. My grandmother, Uncle, Aunts and other family members attended their wedding. I heard it was a big and beautiful wedding up at hospital chapel where my father worked. My grandmother did bring me a piece of their traditional Jamaican wedding cake. We returned to Montego Bay the following day I was about twelve years old.

I entered the United States through Kennedy Airport Saturday, October 16, 1966. I had a two-piece lime green suit made and wore a red cashmere sweater inside. I did not perm my hair because that was strictly forbidden in the church where I had membership. My father specifically sent me money to either perm or hot press my hair before coming to America. Pastor Perry and his wife made it a point to come to my mother's room and lecture me against perming or hot pressing my hair to go to America because that was considered a sin. My mother was in total agreement with them that I should not press or perm my hair because her and my father were still battling for control of me. I was now seventeen and still felt like their pawn. Throughout my life the only time I remember my parents meeting and not fighting about me was at my graduation from Fordham University. (More about that later).

"Country Bumpkin"

When I arrived at Kennedy Airport and my father saw that my hair was not straightened or permed, he became instantly cross. My father told me at Kennedy Airport, "You make me look ashamed, entering the States looking like a country bumpkin." "What will my friends and American neighbors think when they see my daughter with nappy hair?" This was the welcome that I received from my father upon my arrival in America. This was one of those lose-lose situations. I obeyed my mother, the pastor, and his wife which left me in very deep hot water with my father. He did not care what the pastor, his wife, or my mother thought about the way that I looked. He totally rejected the notion that the church or my mother had any right to tell me what to do. That was reserved only for him to dominate and control my life. He wanted me to arrive here looking as if I had already been here. Welcome to America Vivienne!

Why Did You Miss Our Wedding?

When I arrived at their house from the airport, Elsa wanted to know why I didn't attend their wedding. I was stunned. She was upset because she sent me an outfit to wear to their wedding and saw my aunt Mrs. Queen wearing the outfit. I explained that I never knew that an outfit was sent for me to wear to the wedding. Besides, Grammie said that I had to babysit so that they could all go. Elsa said, my grandmother and her daughter Mrs. Queen told her I was behaving as if I was a grown woman and I refused to attend their wedding because I did not like her. I asked Elsa, "to please tell me when the rules between children and adults have changed in Jamaica." Or where in Jamaica can a child under twenty-one tell the adults where they did or did not want to go?" I was looking forward to coming to your wedding, but I was told no. I explained that I did not have clothes because my aunt kept the clothes that were being sent for me by my father. They never made any attempts to get me something to wear and they never told me an outfit came for me to wear. When they assaulted me about not being at their wedding at age seventeen, I was confused, since I was twelve when they were married. I was a child, so why all this anger that I was not there when I had no choice. Who stays angry all those years over something that a child had no control over?

After we had dinner, we all cleaned up and went into the living room. It appears that I was not being believed because my father began to read me his hard-nosed riot act based on a letter my grandmother had written to him when she heard I was coming to America. I was put on restrictions too numerous and too ridiculous to mention. The only thing I could do is to go to work and come home. I felt like I was a hostage in that house. My wicked grandmother had a reason for every evil thing that her and her daughter, Mrs. Queen did to me. My father remained true to his core beliefs that his mother, Grammie, my grandmother was Saint Grammie. In retrospect, in order for my father to accept his mother's behaviors for what they were towards me, he would have to own all that he did against me. The possibility of either of them taking personal responsibility was not on their radars. Most of the people in my father's family thought they were gods unto themselves. They made their own rules, lived by them and whenever they had consequences for their behaviors, they could always find someone else to blame. They never took personal responsibility for the consequences of their behaviors. Even as a child this angered me greatly!

My Education Denied Again

When I received my Greencard, I applied for my social security card. When I said I hadn't graduated high school, the woman told me I could be admitted to high school and receive remedial help to graduate. I would have to be tested first. She told me where the test was being given that day. My reading scores were very high, but I needed remediation in math and other areas. I had been out of school since age fourteen and I had lost a lot of my skills. I was told what high school in Queens was in my area. I immediately given directions and headed to the high school. I wanted to know how I could attend high school there. The white principal told me I could not attend without my parents coming and signing me into school. I was very surprised to see only white teachers, principals and workers there in 1966.

The only black person I saw working there was a janitor. I just thought that was odd. Why there were no black teachers, principals, and other workers in the office like I would have seen in a Jamaican school? When I asked my father about it, he said, blacks in America did not have equal educational opportunities as whites, but Dr. Martin Luther King, Jr. was fighting for change. I mentioned about being able to attend high school, but not about taking the entrance exam or about meeting with the principal. I was told I could go to school at nights and study for my GED, but I had to go to work in the day and provide for myself. In addition, to taking GED classes Tuesday and Thursday nights, I also took remedial classes on Wednesday nights. I worked cleaning houses during the days.

I Began Cutting Again

My cutting behaviors began to surface again shortly after I came to America and was put on restrictions based on my grandmother's lies. I was very upset that I could not go to high school full-time and work part-time. Elsa's niece was attending school full-time and she was being financially supported. She did not work, she went to school, then came home, did chores, and studied. She was being given a platform for her future; I was getting no support for my future. I was required to work and support myself totally and I felt this this was not fair. After the conversation with my father and stepmother, I went into their bathroom and cut myself with one of my father's razor blade that night.

Some of the restrictions conflicted with me attending school three nights a week. I was accused of being pernicious even though I was not. I worked three to five days each week cleaning houses. I sent some money home to my mother whenever I could. I had to pay my father and stepmother for my room and board. I spent a lot of my days off at the library trying to catch up on my skills, but after eighteen months I took the GED Test and failed by eleven points. I was devastated. I felt ashamed. I felt like a failure.

I Will Gut You Like a Rotten Fish

Some time passed and one day when I was off from work my father made breakfast for the both of us and called me to come and eat with him. I thought nothing of it, until he tried to kiss me in the kitchen like he was kissing a woman not a daughter. I was almost twenty. I was no longer the seven-year-old girl he committed incest against almost every night. I loathed the man, but he was my father, so I tried to be civil. I resisted him and he became very angry at me and tried to force himself on me. We began to struggle in the kitchen when I saw a butcher knife laying on the kitchen counter, I picked it up and pointed it at him. My father backed off and I saw and smelled his fear of me. I told my father "I WILL GUT YOU LIKE A ROTTEN FISH", if you EVER came near me like that again." He stepped out of my way. I ran to my room, got my coat and left the house. I went to a nearby park and sat crying, asking." Why does my father hate me so?"

I did not return until late in the evening when I knew everyone would be home and I would be safer. After that incident, I made it a point to leave the house and do a lot of window shopping or go to the library on my days off instead of going home. Whenever I knew no one would be home I stayed away because he often came home for lunch. This made life even more difficult and I received a lot of flak for not wanting to be at home with "the family." I never told anyone about the incident because I did not trust them to believe and support me. My grandmother, Grammie, told them so many lies about me, there was no way for me to defend myself. When I tried to move out on my own to get away from their domination and control, I was accused of wanting to move out so that I become whoring. All I wanted was just to be free of the constant endless turmoil that seemed to say we don't want you here you are not a good fit for us.

My Own Look

After I stopped cleaning houses, I got a job at a department store which worked out great because all the girls in my family was invited to a coming out dance. I was not one of the young women who was being presented, because I had not been able to make any educational accomplishments. It was fun just to be invited to the ball. This was my first ball or formal party and I was excited. I found a beautiful size five spaghetti strap silver brocade gown with a slight train in the back to wear. When I came home everyone thought it was very pretty. I set about to get my accessories. I came home one evening to find one of Elsa's nieces in what I thought was my gown. Well, it was not, she went out and purchased the exact same gown to wear. I was not happy. I wanted my own look for the ball. The next day I returned my gown and purchased a different gown without telling anyone. When I came out of my room in a different gown from hers on the night of the ball, they were not happy. I didn't care! I was very happy that I was able to maintain a look all my own. I did not have to look like someone's twin.

Douglas's Father

Late in 1968 I met Wells. He was a young, handsome Jamaican man and we quickly developed a friendship. He came to my home, met my father, Elsa and relatives who were present before we could begin dating. His story was, he did not know his real father and was raised by a single mother who was in Jamaica. He told me he had an older sister who lived in England and he was here on a student visa attending school to become a draftsman. He also introduced me to some of his family members. His family seem to treat him well and I was treated well also when I was around them.

Poor Decision Making

On one of my days off from working in a nursing home Wells invited me to meet him in the city for lunch. He met me at the train station in Manhattan and took me to lunch. After lunch he claimed he had the afternoon off from school. We saw a movie then we went to hang out at his house. He took me home later that night. We continued seeing each other, until I began to feel sick. I went to see a doctor and he ordered a pregnancy test where I learned that I was pregnant. When I learned that I was pregnant I began to cry because I did not know what I was going to do if he left me.

Nobody Laughing

When I told Wells I was pregnant, he told me to get an abortion. I went into total shock and disbelief. I completely rejected the idea because I believed it was murder of our baby. In our last conversation before we broke up, Wells said to me, "I already have a daughter I do not want another child." "Well, I am not having an abortion, it's our baby." One week later I told my family and my father wanted to see him. I told him we broke up, but I called him and he came to see my father and acknowledge that he was the father of my child. My father told him the advantages of marrying me because I was a legal resident of the United States and he was not. He told my father that my being pregnant was not a reason for us to get married. After he left, my father, said to me: "You are not allowed to live in this house and walk through my gate with a belly showing and no husband. I will help you get an abortion." I said, "NO!" "What do you mean? NO!" "NO!" "Then find somewhere else to live and get out of this house and out of my sight. You are a disgrace to me and this family." Given who my father was, that was a joke for him to take this position about my being pregnant and unmarried, BUT no one was laughing.

Glass Houses

When Wells refused to marry me, my world turned upside down and inside out in an instant on a whole new level. The entire household began to shame and berate me for being pregnant and unmarried. I knew they would all have something to say, but I did not anticipate their degree hatred for me and my unborn child. I knew my behavior of having sex outside of marriage was wrong, but I was not thinking when I went to spend the afternoon with him. What was MOST nauseating to me is that the

TRAUMAS, TRANSFORMATION AND GLORY

women who were calling me names for being pregnant without a husband; were all women who had more than one child with different fathers. Yet, they felt they had the right to pronounce judgment against me for walking where they once did! I learned many years later that Wells was already married with the child he talked about only he assured me he was unmarried. I remember thinking about a cliché we use in Jamaica! "When you live in a glass house, don't throw stones, and if you can't take blows don't throw blows because the stones and blows you throw will come back to you stronger than the ones you threw." Here were women who lived in their own glasses houses in their youth throwing stones at me for being caught in the same glass house they were living in.

The Cultural Stigma

For many Jamaican girls like myself, pregnancy without the benefit of marriage means you are a disgrace to your family. This is a stigma that carries very deep wounds of shame that is often imparted to the child. Many young pregnant Jamaican girls are abandoned and thrown out to manage alone in shame. They and their babies must live out in the streets unless someone takes them in when they are abandoned in their pregnancy. This leads to a life of poverty because of their lack of education. When a girl is pregnant and unmarried in Jamaica, her school days were officially over. My father abandoning my mother and me sent her reeling into the arms of another man who left her with a second and third child. Poverty coupled with more poor choices led to deeper levels of poverty and misery for her and her children. I chose to believe in my heart that if my mother had the means to keep and care for us, she would have. Unfortunately, this is an all too familiar refrain in Jamaican culture. We become casualties because we are unable to change what we are experiencing. It is a vicious cycle that shows no signs of coming to an end in the land of my birth. Jamaica, Jamaica! Jamaica Land I love!

The shame and stigma that comes with being pregnant and unmarried goes deep and can last into the next generation. While we say many things that support marriage before childbearing, and this is good and right. We often do not attach any significance to the traumatizing words of shame that are being transferred through the mother into the unborn child of an unmarried girl or woman. I shudder at the things that were said to my mother and I still cringe at the things that were said to me in my pregnancy. In the late 1950 and 1960 pregnancy without marriage was not acceptable in either Jamaican or American Culture. I know from observation in my culture that many women and men live pure and chaste, yet there is an unchaste, sexually impure spirit that is alive and well in Jamaican and many other cultures today. I am not here to debate the reasons in this book, this is simply an observation for now.

Many years after my son was born, I ran into a woman from church back home. I did not recognize her at first, but she remembered me. I was happy to see someone from there after so many years. However, the reality of my being pregnant and unmarried came front and center like a two-by-four slapping me in my face. Her comment was," I heard about how you disgraced your family and the church. "I heard you had a baby before you were married." She made her comment with the absolutely assurance that I was destined for perdition for my sin of being unmarried and pregnant. It never occurred to her she might find herself in the same inferno because she was so hardcore mean, condemning, and judgmental. I looked at her, smiled, then walked away thinking, you are still "the small mean-spirited stigma police you always were." I later learned and confirmed that all three of her daughters were pregnant before any of them were married. She believed that because she had all her children after she was married that her daughters would be insulated from the unchaste spirit in ours and so many cultures. Her judgmental "small mean-spirited stigma policing" against me and other young Jamaican women came home to roost under her own roof times three.

Thrown out of the House

When I was told that I had to leave my father's house because Wells would not marry me, I went to the bank to withdraw money to rent a room. When I was told I had less than one hundred dollars after saving close to a one thousand dollars I became even more distraught. I asked how this could have happened and I learned that my father withdrew almost all my money. I asked to see the records and I was shown all the times that I made deposits and all the times that my father made withdrawals to support his gambling habit. When I opened the savings account, I was told to put my father's name on my account in case of an emergency. I really did not trust my father, but I was too afraid of the repercussions to say anything.

I went to my father and asked, where is all the money that I have been saving, my account is empty? My father was insulted that I asked him why he used "my money without my permission." He became enraged "Who do you think you are to come and question me about your money. We brought you here from Jamaica, you are downright "out of order, ungrateful, and very disrespectful" to come and ask me such a question." My immediate response was, I didn't ask you to bring me here from Jamaica and I don't owe you anything for doing so. In all of my different employments I had managed to save one thousand dollars and it was gone on the ponies. Elsa wrote to someone in Jamaica who for a monthly support would keep my baby if I went home and left him there after he was born. I said NO! I will not abandon my baby the way that my parents abandoned me! She was not happy that I rejected her solution to keep my child invisible the way that I was when my mother was banished to the country by my father.

I understood that I was in the beginning of the cycle that my mother and so many Jamaican women became caught and trapped in. I wanted out of the cycle, but I did not see any way out at the time for myself or my baby. I only knew I could not have an abortion and I could not send him away. One day while I was at work, one of my coworkers asked me, "Why have you gone from being a fairly happy young girl to a very sad young girl?" I felt that I needed to trust somebody, so I confided and told her what I was going through. I also shared that my father took all the money I saved and used it for gambling. She told me to go to social services and see if they could help me. It was the first time I was hearing about social services. I went there a few days later and spoke to a social worker who believed I had the right to make decisions for me and my baby. They took all my information and said they would get back to me. I left my father's house without telling him where I was going. I stayed with a friend while I continued to work until I was five and half months pregnant.

An Unwed Mother

I entered the home for unwed mothers when I was seven months pregnant. Mine was not a smooth pregnancy. I would just begin to bleed for no apparent reason and the doctors thought I might have a miscarriage, so I was placed on bed rest. I stayed home at my friend's and used what money I saved in the few months after taking my father's name off my account to pay my way. When I entered the home for unwed mothers there were girls who were younger, and some were older. We were required to attend services every morning after breakfast and hear the gospel preached. We were fallen women who needed to be redeemed by the gospel of the Cross. Most of these women were kind and compassionate and the girls on my floor made the best of what we were hearing. I felt at the time that if more focus was placed on my pain rather than my being unmarried and pregnant, I may have been able to connect with them and the gospel they were preaching. I knew I was a sinner; we all knew we had done wrong. I was riddled with shame, guilt, feeling a world of hurt, unloved from as far back as I could remember. I felt that I was being presented with a gospel about an ethereal God who was too far away from the reality of my world to connect with me. I needed a gospel that was about the love and compassion of Jesus Christ that would redeem me without further penalty or penance for my sin. It is that gospel that eventually brought me to Christ and got me to stay.

Douglas' Birth

I was in my room sitting on my bed talking with my roommate one night when in the middle of our conversation I felt something crawling on my feet. When I looked down it was a mouse. I was afraid of mouse because of my encounter them when I slept under the cellar to avoid a beating from Uncle David. When I saw the mouse I began to scream, jumped off my bed and began having contractions with blood running down my legs. My roommate called the emergency number and I was taken to the hospital. It took twenty-two hours for Douglas to born because he was in a breach position of feet first. I was bleeding with each contraction during labor. My mother told me she came home from work in Jamaica and prayed until late in the morning for me. My son was born early on a Thursday morning.

When I entered the home for unwed mothers my intentions were to put my son up for adoption so that he would have two parents. Birth mothers were not allowed to see the child they were putting up for adoption at that time. I was having second thoughts about his adoption, but I did not say anything to anyone. I asked if I could see my son after he was born and was told no, he is going up for adoption. I climb out of bed and walked down to the new-born nursery and begged the nurse to just let me see and hold him and she relented. When I saw my son and held my son my heart became so filled with love for him that I began to weep, and I could not let him go. My social worker came to see me in the hospital and told me she contacted my father to say I had delivered a baby boy successfully. My son was born on October 23, 1969. The social worker told me they offered to have me come back home only after I signed an agreement that the baby's father could not come to their house. I had no idea where he was. One of his relatives told me that he went to Canada out of fear that I or my father might have him deported. I told the social worker, what they really mean is, they do not want me or my baby because I have disgraced them. It was only about them and how they looked in the eyes of those they wanted to impress. The risk of signing their agreement was that if he should happen to show up without my knowing I would be thrown out of the house again. This time with my infant son. I could not risk trusting them not turning on me again.

I Want to Keep My Baby

Seeing and holding my son was a turning point in my life. I still had no place to go and I had no money and no support. My social worker quickly come up with a new plan and told the adoptive parents that the birth mother changed her mind. I was discharged back to the home and my son was placed in emergency Foster Care. Shortly after my son was born my mother came to America living in the city. I called her and she said I could come and stay with her until I was able to make plans. I was leery, because we had not been able to bond as I got older. However, being desperate I took her up on the offer and three weeks after I gave birth, I was working as a receptionist part-time. I would travel from the Bronx to the Queens every other week to spend only one hour with Douglas. I did not want to become a welfare mother. I was afraid that if I went on welfare, I might fall deeper into the cycle I was struggling to get out of.

A New Social Worker

I was assigned a new social worker named Mrs. Elliot, she was African American, and we made a healthy professional connection. She did not appear to judge me because of my poor choice of sexual immorality. We came up with a plan that I should get an education where I could be gainfully employed without a high school diploma. I took a ten-month course in secretarial studies which started in January 1970. I applied for a student loan for one thousand dollars and was accepted into a secretarial and finishing school. I paid it all back. I still kept seeing my son, but it was hard to leave my baby after each visit. One month I was too sick to go and when I saw him the following month, he did not recognize me and would not let me hold him for about thirty minutes into our visit. He was an infant and that was a natural part of his development, but it broke my heart. I got a job at Department Store in the Square area to pay my mother room and board and travel expenses. At secretarial school they taught me secretarial skills, how to apply makeup, and how to dress for business. I doubled my efforts after the incident of my son not knowing me and graduated in eight months with a Junior Secretarial Diploma.

Junior Secretary

That August I became employed in Harlem as a junior secretary for a woman who was a proposal writer. For me to be employed as a Junior Secretary was tremendous, considering how many adults in my life wrote me off as the girl least likely to succeed. One of my teacher's at senior school said that to me because I was always late for school. Mrs. Elliot, the social worker visited us and told my mother that if we were to get an apartment together it would speed up the process of me getting Douglas out of Foster Care. We pooled our monies together and got a two-bedroom apartment and purchased used furniture for the entire apartment. I put a down payment on a new youth bed, a toy chest with a dresser for Douglas before he came home. Douglas could not come home until our apartment passed inspection and daycare was in place for him. By the time my son came home he was a year old. I was very proud of myself because I did not totally abandon my son the way that I was abandoned by both my parents. I pulled it off with help from the God I did not want. I got my son out of Foster Care in one year.

CHAPTER SIX

HOPING FOR A FUTURE

My former husband and I met while we worked together in the same department store. Our relationship was a rocky one based solely on his physical needs and my great need to be loved outside of God's order. Being loved in a godly way is something I knew nothing about growing up. His need for physical gratification was intense. It was only later after we were married that I found out he was addicted to pornography. I was uncomfortable meeting these need of his because we were not married, but I felt that I could not keep him if I said no to his demands. While I knew him during my pregnancy, we did not begin our relationship until after my son Douglas was born. I felt like I was damaged goods and did not believe anyone else would want me. When he began to pay attention to me, I was too easily flattered, he was saying things to me that no one else ever said. He would say that I was pretty, that I had a great slim body, and he like my luscious behind. He continued to flatter me about the way I dressed. I met his mother shortly before she died of lung cancer. His mother seemed to like me a lot. I felt like I was his trophy while we were dating. The issue with hunting for a trophy is, as soon as it has been acquired it is placed on a shelf to be ignored.

We dated for over a year before we were married, and he treated me well. I still never felt that he really loved me or if he loved me, why? What was there about me that he loved? Meeting his intense physical needs seemed to be what he loved the most about me. He and I went out on weekends to house parties, movies, plays, and out to eat. We had picnics in Central Park alone and attended the Summer Concerts. He proposed on a Friday night after taking me out to dinner. When he asked me to marry him, I said, yes! I viewed his proposal as a chance to make a life for us and to have a family, something I desperately wanted. In addition, when I was abandoned by Wells and my father, he was someone whom I could call while in the home for support which I saw as a good character trait. Someone who would be there for me as I was for him when he lost his mother. Prior to getting married I had a concern about his womanizing because we both grew up in a culture where it is pandemic. I saw many marriages and children being hurt by men and women who were not faithful in their marriage covenant. Many of the men I knew growing up had what was called outside children. I was an outside child, so I was no stranger to the problems and intense hardships and isolation of these relationships.

Life Was only About My Father

After we made our wedding announcement to both of our families we began to plan. Well I did most of the planning while he seemed to be along for the ride. I wanted to move back to the suburbs, but he wanted to live in the city, and we spoke about owning our own home someday. He felt that since he was a bookkeeper, he was the logical choice to handle our finances taking care of all the bills after we were married. We would combine our incomes and each of us would have the same amount for our weekly allowance. After what happened with my father stealing my money, I was nervous, but decided I should trust him in-spite of my feelings.

As our wedding plans progressed, we quickly ran into difficulty that we were never able to overcome. At the time we became engaged I was living with my mother. When we met with my father and he offered to pay for all the food with the cake included. We felt that all three sets of parents should be included on our wedding invitations. When the invitations were sent out, my father objected to any other name being on the invitation except his. He wanted top billing with the invitations having his name as the only parent. This was the beginning of a process where my father refused to accept that he alone could not be on the invitation and refused to attend our wedding or to pay for the purchase of the food unless we gave him his way with the invitations.

My Wedding Day

There was no love lost between me and my father, but I really needed him to come through for me. While my mother did not think that I should marry him because she felt that he would abuse me as soon as he placed a ring on my finger but, she did support me to be married. I had my doubts about him loving me, but I really felt that because he had been supportive of me and I was also supportive of him in crisis we would find a way to stay married. However, on the night before our wedding I could not sleep. I felt a sense of terror about marrying him that I had no language to describe. When I met with my bridal party at the beauty parlor for our hair appointments the following day, I was a nervous wreck. I was crying, feeling fearful, and wanted to call the wedding off.

When I went to call my fiancé and tell him I was sorry we could not get married, I allowed myself to be talked out of it. I called my father and he said he had not changed his mind he was not coming because he felt dishonored. When I got home from the hairdresser, I called my mother into her room and told I was changing my mind and calling the wedding off. My mother became very angry. After all I have been telling you not to marry him, now on the day of your wedding you want to call it off. The photographer is sitting in the living room. Everything is ready, people are already at the church. "What am I going to tell everybody?" I went into my room and my friends helped me dress, the photographer helped me to laugh. I put my terrors aside and we got married because I again did not have language to say why I felt the way that I did nor the courage to say no.

We were married on December 4, 1971 in the Bronx, New York. When we were planning our wedding, he was put in charge of making all the reservations for our honeymoon in the Poconos.

I made some preliminary inquiry and passed the information on to him. He assured me that he made all the reservations, "I took care of everything." We were taking the short flight from LaGuardia Airport and we were to be picked up and driven to the resort. After our wedding, we went back to the apartment to change and his best man was driving us to the airport. When we got to the apartment, I asked him to carry me over the threshold and he refused. I stood at the door until he carried me over the threshold. I was only one hundred and thirty-five pounds so being overweight was not an issue. His friend drove us to the airport, however when we went to check in for our flight, there were NO reservations for us. For me this was a major deliberate error on his part. He knew he did not make the reservation and yet he went along with the charade of being driven to the airport only to be embarrassed.

For Worse

The issue was not a lack of money, it was a lack of the value that he placed on our marriage. Why was I worth less to him now that we were marred? I believed that he married me because he knew he could not continue to have a physical relationship with me if we stayed single. I felt he wanted to marry me, yet he did not see me as someone that he should respect, honor and value. I felt completely deflated and humiliated, that I was now married to a man who cared so little for the well-being of our marriage that he lied about the honeymoon arrangements. This became a significant beginning of how he would conduct himself throughout our marriage by neglecting our family life together. We already had an apartment that was completely furnished. Douglas's room was ready when we picked him up from his godmother. However, the lights were not scheduled to be turned until the following week.

He came up with the lame idea that we should go to Washington D. C. for our honeymoon weekend. I went along because I did not want to go home with him at this point. We spent the night at the nation's capital, went to dinner on Sunday evening and came home on Monday. We had both taken the week off from work, so we made the most of fixing up the apartment. My son Douglas stayed with his godmother in Queens during the wedding since we were going away for a week. (Ha, ha.) When we came home, I made another vow to myself. Now that I was already married, I needed to make it work even if it killed me. It almost did.

He Denied My Son

We went to Queens on the train and brought Douglas home. On the way home a friend of his saw us together with Douglas on the train. She commented, "Oh, I did not know you had a son?" "He looked at her and said, that is not my son he's my wife's son. Now, that was and is true. I looked at him and moved with my son and sat in another seat. He wanted to know why I was upset, I said we are married and if the situation was reversed, I would not have said that in deference to your feelings. He apologized, but we were married less than a week and he was showing his true character at a rapid pace. More to the point he was showing me the character I did not allow myself to see while we were dating. To me, he had stopped trying to be what he felt he needed to be to get me now that he had me. I made it a point not to ask too much of him when it came to Douglas. Before we were married, he told people that Douglas was his son, but that all changed once we were married. After we were married about a year it became an issue for us to go out as a couple or as a family together. After this incident of him denying my son, he decided that he should adopt my son giving him his last name and I agreed.

My Brother Died in Jamaica

My fourteen-year-old brother Samuel became sick and diagnosed with acute Leukemia. My mother was devastated by this news and wanted me to go to Jamaica with her, but he said no. When she came back the news was not good because his illness was in the final stages. My brother called me one night from Jamaica and asked me to come and see him. After I got off the phone, I told him I really needed to go to Jamaica because I felt it was a final request from my brother. So, I made plans and I took Douglas with me; he was almost four years old at the time. The day after

I got to Jamaica, I went to the hospital to seem him. The doctors said he needed a miracle if he was going to live.

After I was there a week visiting him every day, I went to see him very early one morning, cleaned him up and gave him his breakfast. He told me he wanted to see Aunt Inez who was caring for my siblings at the time while my mother was here in the United States. Aunt Inez did not have a telephone, so I took a cab to the house to take her back to see him. I felt it was urgent. When I got to the house, they were all crying. The hospital called a neighbor and when Aunt Inez went to the phone, they told her that my brother died five minutes after I said goodbye. I called my mother and my sister in the States to say that Samuel died. This was a very sad time for my family.

I called my husband later that evening and told him my brother died and I needed to stay longer than ten days to attend his funeral. He became angry. "Why does your family have to always do things like this?" "Do things like what? My fourteen-year-old brother just died of Leukemia and my family is in crisis. When your mother was ill and after she died, I supported you and your family, and I did not give you any grief." How dare you? I asked him to come to Jamaica to join me and my family, but he refused. It was not a money issue and he could have taken time off from work. My family asked me when he was coming to the funeral and I lied because I felt such shame over his behaviors. They had watched me tirelessly support him during times of crisis in his family and now he was not available for me or my family in our crisis.

Brother's Funeral

However, when I got home, he was angry and began to accuse me of taking advantage of him because he allowed me to go to Jamaica. I should have put a stop to his increasing control over me then, but at the time it seemed foolish to have to justify myself in this matter concerning the death of my brother. He was distant when I came home, and I remember asking him if he had been with another woman in the short while that I was gone. He claimed he had not. I also said, we used to be able to talk things through, but I don't know what is eating you. I don't know how to read minds. Since the day that we said I do, you have been a different man. You just don't understand me was his angry reply! No, I have not misunderstood, you are very different from the man I thought I was marrying. It's not just a small change which I fully expected." This is where he would retreat behind the newspapers. Whenever, he picked up the newspaper is was useless trying to talk with him.

Pregnant Again

A few months after returning from my brother's funeral I learned that I was pregnant. My husband was very happy that we were finally pregnant, and I was happy to be having another baby. Considering the doctor's report that I would not conceive or carry a child to term because of scar tissues, I was pregnant again. I began to gain weight very rapidly in my second trimester, my blood pressure was unusually high, and they found protein in my urine. My doctor said I had something called Preeclampsia. I was in the sixth month of my pregnancy by now, so he wanted me to stop working and go on bed rest in April. I was due in June. Well, my husband being a man of extreme frugality felt I should stay at work so that the insurance would no pause in our coverage. He also had insurance, but if both our insurances were to be billed, we would not have any bills. My health and the health of our baby was at risk, so I told my job to take the three months insurance payment out of my paycheck so that both insurances would cover us and took maternity leave early.

While I was pregnant with our son Graham, one of his friends called him asking to borrow money for a down payment on a car. I said no to his request for the loan. However, later that week when I went to the bank, I noticed that our savings account balance was short in the amount his friend asked to borrow. When I came home and asked him why our account was missing that amount, he told me he gave the money to his friend. I was angry because that was not only his money and I was opposed to the loan. My husband became enraged at me and before I could complete my sentence, I was backed into a corner and threatened. I was told to shut up and mind my business. When he pushed in the corner of our bedroom screaming in my face, I had a flashback of Cousin Beasley pushing me in the corner of his room and raping me with his hand over my mouth. I spoke back and said, "When I work and help us to save money it is my business where it goes, and I have a right to have my opinion honored." He told me he was the man and his rules were higher than mine. After this argument I began to vomit violently as I began to feel lost on a level I had not experienced before this.

During my pregnancy I began to feel a greater sense of being intimidated by him that was difficult to explain to myself let alone to others. I found myself backing off more and more for fear of him hurting me physically while I was pregnant and after. Part of my difficulty in the marriage is that my mother told me not to marry this man because he was going to abuse me. Therefore, when his abusive behaviors continued to escalate, I was too ashamed to tell my family I was in big trouble. I kept putting on a front and lying to cover the problems. It was during our pregnancy that he began to introduce pornography into our marriage. I was totally against this and rejected the idea as part of my life or his. By the time our son Graham was born, we were having some serious issues with womanizing, pornography, his control of me and our finances. I did not have the language to express any of what I was experiencing, so silence seemed best.

Custody of Princess

When his mother died, he had a younger sister who was underage and being raised by his mother and stepfather before she died. He was the only father that she knew, and he did treat her well. However, he remarried within six months following the death of their mother. This was an immediate problem as his sister Princess had difficulty adjusting to this new situation while she was still grieving the loss of her mother. I was two months pregnant with Graham when I received the first call from the police and social worker. The social worker also informed us that his younger sister was in their custody because of a family dispute.

The stepfather's new wife in an argument with Princess picked up a machete and began to threaten her. Princess ran out of the house and was chased down the block by this adult waving the machete at the child. A neighbor watching the scene of a woman chasing as child with a machete called the police. They were scheduled to go to Juvenile Court on a Wednesday and wanted one of her two older brothers to come to court and take custody of her. They both refused to become involved with the issue. His mother's sister went, but the arrangement did not last very long and they were back in court before long.

My husband still refused to get involved, because at his mother's death she made not arrangements in her will to provide for the care of her daughter. When his mother died the stepfather was in possession of the house and everything else that they owned. He did not provide an inheritance to any of her children from her assets in the marriage. When Princess was back in court after being thrown out by her aunt he still refused to stand up for his sister. She was in the eleventh grade by this time. She was not treated very well by the aunt's family and I would receive frequent calls to help mend the fences between them. A few days before the second court date I received a call, so I gave the phone to her brother. He handed it back to me. The social worker wanted to speak with me and not him. She gave me all of the information for the hearing and asked me to try and persuade him to be in court.

After dinner I cleaned up the kitchen and tried to make an appeal to him as her older brother. I offered to have her come and live with us at least until she was eighteen where she would go off to college. She was a very bright girl and I just did not want to see her thrown away like I was. He refused to relent. So early the next morning I told him I would go and take custody of his sister and asked him to come with me. He said. NO! He told me before I left for court, if you take custody of her, she will be your responsibility not mine and he kept his word. So, after I got Douglas off the school, I called my supervisor and told her I had a family emergency and would not be in. I rode the trains from the city out to the suburbs, met the social worker. I was five months pregnant by now with Graham.

She asked me where my husband was. I told her he was not coming, but if I would do, I will take custody of Princess. The social worker told me she was hoping that someone would stand up. Every family member that she called refused to get involved. Well she got to my heart, because I remember being mistreated as a girl and young woman growing up. They gave me a check that day after court, which I cashed and used for her. I got her a bed with a dresser and as many necessities as we could purchase, and I gave her an allowance. The following day I called in again, took all the paperwork they gave me and enrolled her in high school. She graduated high school and went to college for a two-year secretarial degree.

Chapter Seven

Did We Get Rid of "The Belly?"

After Graham was born my husband made it clear that he did not want any more children. I reminded him of our agreement to have two children of our own, but he refused to discuss it. When I mentioned that I would like us to consider trying again for another child I got such a cold stare from him that my spine felt stiff. I decided to go along, not to rock the boat since our marriage was very rocky. My body kept rejecting the inter-uterine devices, so I was placed on a low dose of birth control pill. Despite taking the pill I became pregnant again. I was surprised and excited because I wanted a daughter.

Another Baby

I began to think through and developed a plan to announce that we were expecting again. I decided that I would plan a special candlelight dinner for us the night I broke the news to him. That day I took off from work and made sure that he would be home early. My husband rarely came home early, and I put myself at risk for abuse if I asked him where he was or why he was out so late. I got the boys bathed and fed and read to them then put them to bed. I decided that I would do what was called a fondue meal. I shopped and secured all that I would need to make the night special. I made his favorite meat, sauces, salad, and deserts and had the red wine that he liked. I even a purchased a special outfit for the occasion of announcing of the birth of our third child. I set the table with my best china, flatware, and candles. The scene was ready for my big announcement.

No! Get an Abortion

When he arrived home the fondue pot was heated with peanut oil and I was ready to serve him his meal after which I would present my case to keep our baby. I asked him to wait until dinner was over to hear our wonderful news. I made a short speech about the importance of our family. Then I told my husband that we were pregnant again and waited for his response. He sat with very cold depraved indifference and said to me, NO! I took you with one child and I have changed my mind we are only having two children. Call your doctor and schedule an abortion because we are not having another child. If you insist on having this baby, you will be on your own because I will leave you and them. He got up went into the living room and turned on the television.

I was stunned with disbelief! I knew there would be a difference of opinion, but this totally caught me off guard, it was as if I had been kicked in the heart. I had a lot of experience with his overt cruelty after we were married. This was his baby and I did nothing to deliberately get pregnant. I was his wife and he just sat in the most matter-of-fact way and instructed me to terminate the life of our baby. His manner about our baby, was as if he was talking about swatting a fly, stomping a cockroach, or killing a mosquito. I was mortified. He knew all too well that my oldest sons' father Wells and my biological father abandoned me when I would not abort Douglas. This made his response to me even more innately cruel and betraying. Then he called out to me from the living saying, after all, we are not breaking the law anymore. I had never heard or seen him that cold. I felt that my heart was being torn to pieces from hearing him say get an abortion we are not breaking any law. Abortion had become legal and he felt that the legality of abortion meant we would have no consequences for our actions. That I disagreed with us aborting our baby did not matter to him.

My biggest fear in telling him I was pregnant was that he might physically abuse me which would lead to a miscarriage. When tears began to roll down my face, he looked at me and told me my tears could not convince him otherwise. I laid next to him and wept throughout the night. He rolled over and went to sleep. I mourned, whimpered, sobbed and slipped into a quiet state of despair. In the morning after he was dressed for work, he confirmed his words to me once again. If you do not have the abortion you will be raising the children by yourself because I will be leaving you. He said, "Listen to you with all that crying." You are not capable of raising children by yourself, because you are too weak!" I called in sick that morning, took Douglas to kindergarten and kept Graham who was nine months old at home with me.

Plunged into Depression

I was no stranger to depression, cutting and other numbing behaviors, but not while pregnant. After all my planning his response plunged me into a deeper depression than when I was pregnant with Douglas. During the course of the day my past, with the same issue, came back to haunt me like a tormenting Greek chorus. Being married to him since 1971, 1 knew that his statement about leaving us if we did not abort was a real promise rather than an idle threat. The man that proposed to me on that Friday night, who said he loved me and was committed to till death do us part, was leaving me unless we aborted our baby. I thought Vivienne you are such a fool, what made you think that he was any different from Wells or your father. He is just as self-centered as they both were. Different than what? Better than who? I was abandoned all over again and I had no idea how I had placed myself into the same situation twice. Love and marriage offered neither me nor my children any protection from abandonment of being told to abort our baby. His statement that he took me with one child brought me back to that place where I wondered if he really loved me. The mindset that he considered me to be less than he was, less deserving of his love and time once we were married. That nagging sense that terrorized me the night before our wedding was playing out in a frightening drama even my imagination could not conjure up.

The Deep Pain of Being Ignored by My Husband

During the time that my husband kept vexing me to abort our baby, he never made love to me, never kissed, touched me, and ignored me even more than he did before. He would walk into the apartment and act as if I was not even there. He refused to answer me whenever I asked him any question. I did not feel stable in our marital relationship, but his actions totally de-stabilized me. I developed intensified feelings of hatred for him. As much as I hated him, I hated myself more for marrying him and for not leaving after we were married, and he showed his true character. He would call me at work daily asking me if I made the appointment, "to get rid of the belly yet." After what seemed like an eternity of endless weeping and his refusal to relent over us getting the abortion; I finally called my OB/GYN and made an appointment. When I told him what we wanted to do he said that the surgery would be handled as a same day surgery at the hospital.

"Frozen Feelings"

On the morning of the abortion a friend came by and watched my children for me. I asked her not to tell my mother that I was having an abortion. The place that God had created to be a safe haven of nurture of our baby was the place where our baby died. I was convinced that this was the daughter that I wanted. He warned not to discuss the abortion with my mother or family, and I did not take them into my confidence. My real fear was that my mother would pronounce judgment against me if she knew. We drove in silence into the city where no glances no looks were exchanged between us as we traveled to kill our baby. I could feel my heart breaking and I wanted to jump from the moving car several times. In his demand for the abortion, we were now total strangers. The gulf between us was fixed and as wide and deep as the Grand Cannon.

Finality of Marriage

I wondered why I felt such finality about us, but I was unable to express the overwhelming feelings of pain. We prearranged that he would park across the street and come into the hospital and wait until I was out of surgery. When I asked him how long it would take to get back from parking the car, he told me that he was not coming to surgery with me. Why not? You agreed that you would and now you have changed your mind without telling me until now. I am not the one who placed this baby in my belly, and I should not be doing this alone. He sharply and angrily said, if you are still pregnant when I come to pick you up later today my bags will be packed, and I will leave you for good. Who do you think will want you with three children? He then put the car in drive, pulled out into traffic and drove away. After he drove away and left me standing there all alone I walked, for what seemed like a mile, as I walked to the floor where abortions were performed, I felt as if my unborn baby and children were being torn to pieces by his cruel behaviors against us. I took the elevator upstairs and checked in at the front desk. I had heard about this floor in the hospital while I was at work. I had no reason to believe that I would someday be on that very floor aborting our unborn baby. The floor had a certain sense of foreboding; it was cold, and appeared to be uncaring and unfeeling, barren of life, in-spite of the attempts to decorate it cheerfully. The paint on the wall was off white but is appeared a dull gray to me as I looked around.

After the Abortion

Following the abortion, they gave me prescriptions for pain and antibiotics. I took the antibiotics, but not the pain medication. I felt that I deserved to be punished. I also felt that we would both burn in perdition for taking our own baby's life. So, I allowed myself to feel the post-abortion pain and guilt, but not the grief. After the aborting of our baby, I felt frozen inside on a much deeper level than when I was growing up in Montego Bay. I would hide in the bathroom and cut myself to relieve the pain of my "frozen feeling." My baby died BUT, my surgery was successful. It struck me as wholly unnerving that the abortion staff never said to me your baby died. He or she did not suffer in the procedure. Only that "your surgery went well." How Sanitized, I thought!

The Whole Point of Legalized Abortion

I remembered thinking to myself, my surgery went well, but the patient died, but the mother lived. Wasn't that the "whole" point of legalized abortions? This is what my precious little baby girl was reduced to, "my surgery went well." Those words seem to ring hollow, empty, and surreal in my heart then and years later as I have developed a fuller awareness of our actions. Abortion is much more than we made a choice based on the legality of our civil rights. The baby we aborted had a purpose on the planet, a God given design that would be life-giving to a specific portion of the world. What we both did in our choice ended all possibility of her purpose being manifested. For even if someone else is born later and is given our baby's design, they will not perform the way that our child was designed to perform it.

"Did You Get RID of the Belly?"

When he picked me up at the hospital that evening, he only wanted to know, "Did you get rid of the belly?" Yes! He never asked me how I was feeling, or if I was in pain it did not matter to him. The "belly" was gone, and he was happy. As I looked at him, he was no longer the man I loved and married, he was vulgar stench in my nostrils. I rode home with him in quiet despair that he did not seem to notice. All that mattered to him was, "the belly was gone." When I got home, he made-an-attempt to help me out of the car and I asked him not to touch me. I wanted to vomit violently all over him. Prior to my having the abortion he had refused to touch me or make love to me or show me any form of affection. Now that his demand to "get rid of the belly" was accomplished he wanted to pretend as if he was kind and caring. I wanted none of it, I did not want to be touched by him, yet I was still married to him even if he was not married to me.

These painful feelings were buried alive for decades so that I could appear to be functioning well. I felt such an overwhelming grief, my spirit, and soul cried. Unless you have had an abortion there is no real way for you to know how the pain, grief, shame, and spirit wounding from this self-inflicted trauma will play out in your life. It is impossible to walk in the shoe of someone who have aborted a baby, if you have not. Likewise, it is impossible to crawl inside someone and understand why they made abortion their choice. This requires complex rather than simple thinking process because of where fear and the enemy's lies take us. When it comes to this issue there are too many shades of grey to judge the individual who embraced choice. We can and do make our judgments against women who have aborted their babies, but it is wholly unfair, unreasonable, and unjust for us to do so because sinner's sin and Christ died for all sins who have sinned and fallen short of the glory of God. You can argue, I would never have aborted my baby no matter what! But haven't you killed someone's reputation, destiny, purpose, design, or chances of a good marriage with your tongue.

Did We Have the Right?

All nations provide civil authorities with the responsibility for the protection of human life which includes the life of the unborn. Out of our civil responsibility we are to secure and safeguard the sanctity of all human life. Man is not individually to avenge death because human life is a gift from God which man cannot rightly dispose of unless and except as God permits it. The real issue in our abortion is the condition of our hearts not the abortion law of choice. Should "choice" be repealed, it would change nothing. Women have been having abortion before the laws made it legal and will continue to do so. It's a heart issue. He was fundamentally as lawless, as corrupt, and morally bankrupt as my father and Douglas's father ever was. My heart on the other hand was so traumatized that all I could see was my desperate need to protect myself from being abandoned another time and to have the legitimacy of belonging to someone; because I did not belong to myself or to God. Somewhere in the process of being traumatized repeatedly my conscience became charred. While this is in fact the truth, it still did not remove my responsibility to safeguard the life of my innocent unborn baby. I failed to keep her safe for the design, destiny, and purposes of God. In answer to my own question did we have the Right to "Get Rid of the Belly/ BABY?" "NO" While we had the right of civil law of "choice, we had no divine authority or dominion mandate to wipe out an entire generation from our lineage that was a gift from God.

Obstacles to Post Abortion Grief

Following the act of aborting our baby I could not grieve for me or my baby. Abortion is a traumatic event in the lives of the family every aspect of our lives. Abortion only appears to be a singular event, but everyone who is attached to us suffered a loss even if they never knew we had an abortion. My sons are missing their sister. My sister-in-law is missing a niece. The list of who is missing what is endless when there is a death of a baby in the family no matter how the baby died. There is no open forum to grieve an abortion. This grief is not an acceptable form of grief even in a society where it is legal because of the self-traumatizing nature of the event. I felt engulfed in the suffering our unborn baby, yet I could not give myself permission to grieve. The reason only I could give myself permission to grieve is because no one else is responsible to do so for me. My inability to grieve left me frozen in the infancy of aborting our baby. I never stopped wondering, who my baby would grow up to be. Where she would go to college? Who she would marry? How many children she would have? What would our relationship be like as mother and daughter? Would she trust me to tell me she wanted to abort my grandchild? When I see, hear and think about Douglas and my only grandchild, I am still filled with regrets that I did not tell my husband to pack his bags and take a long walk off a short plank over deep waters.

Separate and Alone

Although he and I lived in the same house and shared some familiar things, we lived very separate lives. His womanizing and pornography increased after the abortion, so did his drinking as well as my depression and suicidal thoughts. I told him one night that I would totally refuse physical intimacy with him if he brought the issue of us engaging in pornography up to me again in our marriage. No matter how many times I tried to explain to him that I felt humiliated and degraded by pornography he could not hear me. His twisted appetite led to our first physical separation. Each adulterous affair that he had took him to a deeper level of depravity concerning my well-being. He brought home an STI with a new twist. After he learned he was infected he went to another doctor rather than our family physician. He got himself tested, treated then avoided being with me physically because he would be re-infected. His only thought was to protect himself. He made no effort to protect me or to help me get treatment ahead of time. One night I was doubled over in pain and he took me to the emergency at my mother's insistence. I was treated and cultures were taken. I was given pain medication and antibiotics. On our way home I said, "What have you given me?" He went into his silent act. My mother stopped by to see me the following day and wondered if my husband was working obeah/witchcraft against me. Several days later I received a call from my gynecologist telling me I needed further treatment from my visit to the emergency room because I had an STI.

I refused to have any intimate contact with him which created tension and violence between us at nights to where I slept on the couch. He complained that I put him on punishment. After several weeks he finally agreed to use protection in all of our intimate encounters, but it was a constant tug-of- war. It was at this point that I left to spend the weekend at a friend's. My departure was not planned, and I realized that leaving a husband with two children and a teen-age-sister-in-law needed a strongly developed plan. My husband paid me a visit while I was away and asked me to let us try again. I said I would return only if he agreed to go with me to marriage counseling.

Counselor Betrayal

When I got back to our apartment after our brief separation, I began to discuss with him our need for counseling. He told me that his marriage was a happy one and he did not know what my problem was or why my marriage was unhappy. I said, I am happy for you that you are in a happy marriage. However, the marriage that I am in with you, is wretched and there needed to change, or we cannot survive. I explained that I wanted the two of us to at least make efforts to move and grow in the same directions to give our sons a better family life. The marriage we had, I was with the children alone, while he lived as if, and he was still a single man sowing his "wild oats." He was always absent from our family gatherings. When I insisted that he attend a family function, I was made to feel guilty for wanting him to be with his family. Although he agreed to go for counseling before I came back home, he was searching for a way out of it now that I was back home. So, he came up with a list of counselor requirements that he felt would be impossible to meet.

I found a counselor who was, male and Jamaican as he requested. So we scheduled an appointment and began marriage counseling, but by our third counseling session he wanted out. I told him on our way home if you no longer want to be in counseling, you tell the counselor why you feel you don't need it. So, he came up with a plot to sabotage the process and it worked, but in the long run cost him everything. He called the counselor to say he needed to speak with him alone. My husband never told me that he had contacted our counselor to set-up his own arrangement. I only learned of this when we arrived for our session that day.

Special Session

When I went into the session with him after his special time alone with our counselor, I was under attack from the counselor. My husband told our counselor that I was refusing to be intimate with and that is why he was having all these adulterous affairs and viewing pornography. I was outraged! I confronted him and the counselor in the same session. I explained that the period that I had refused him intimacy after he gave me an STI and refused to use protection. This was not his first STI and I wanted us to use protection before we resume any intimacy which he finally admitted. The counselor backed off, but it was too easy for him to sabotage the process.

After my confrontation he acknowledged to the counselor that he was not telling the truth that he had access to me whenever he wanted before the STI. He also finally admitted I was not frigid and a great intimate partner, but that he loved what he referred to as dirty films and magazines that are major issues, for "her" pointing to me. He told the counselor that he wanted to be with other women as well as his wife. The counselor asked him, how do you plan on maintain your marriage with your womanizing behaviors. My husband replied he did not believe it should be such a big deal to me. It is a very big, big deal for me, I interrupted. We left the session early and drove most of the way home in silence. When we reached upper Manhattan, he began to pull the car over to the curb and I became terrified.

While I felt safe enough to confront him on his lies in the counselor's office. I was very concerned about what he might do when we got home. There his real anger would be without the presence of another male to keep him from exploding. My initial thoughts were, Jesus, this man is going to beat me down in the streets kill me, and my family will bury me soon. Who will raise my children? However, he went into his cold-hearted dialogue. "I am your husband. As your husband I have the right to be with any woman I want that is available to me! As my wife you are to grin and bear it. IF you had been raised to be a good Jamaican woman, it would not be a problem for you because this is what Jamaican men do." I thought to myself, really!

All Jamaican Men are Not Womanizers

I disagreed with him that ALL Jamaican men cheat on their wives. It is culturally endured by women because of the lack of economic empowerment in Jamaica as I was growing up as a girl for many women. For although I lived in America and worked, he controlled my personal finances. I reminded him that we discussed these issues of being faithful in our marriage. I promised I would not keep myself from you and I have kept my promise in spite of your womanizing. I wanted a husband who was faithful in all areas of our marriage. My husband stated that he did not plan to stop being a womanizer and I could not do anything about it. Internally I agreed I could not stop him because I am not the kind of woman who wants to control how a man behaves towards me. I was a good wife to him by my choice and I wanted the same from him.

When I must make a man honor and respect me, it is neither honor nor respect it is degradation. I looked after our children and took his sister in because it was the right thing to do. I knew without any doubt that without a miracle from God our marriage was over. Yet, because I allowed him to force me into having our abortion, I felt that God would not listen to me, so I stayed clear of going anywhere near God for help. Looking back, I can see His fingerprint all over my life, but at that time I was too blinded in pain to see anything else. I knew I needed to prepare myself for a break-up with him. The problem was he controlled all the financial power in the marriage including my paycheck.

Chapter Eight

Taking Back My Power

As my marriage digressed a very deep sense of helplessness engulfed me. I needed to leave, but how? Where could I go? What would I use for money? Where would I be safe? I thought the first thing I needed to do was to get control of the money I was making. While I knew it was vitally necessary, I could not see how it would be possible. I finally got enough courage to stand up and take back my financial freedom. I made up in my mind that if we had to fight physically, so let it be. It was quite messy, but I held my ground until after several days we divided up the bills. We decided what we would both pay from our individual salaries. I made him take the rent and larger bills, while I took on what I called the smaller essentials.

Prior to this point he would dole out an allowance to me as if I was his child. Whenever I needed to purchase anything for the house, kids, or myself, it would lead to an argument where I had to justify the needs before I was granted permission to spend our money. He invested our money in pornography and other women. In Jamaican culture these behaviors are called investing in hairy banks. Hairy bank is a reference to men, especially married men, who invest their time, substance, and money in outside relationships. These relationships often produced outside children that they are required to support financially. The married wife feels that her children are entitled to the lion's share of her husband's substance, and rightly so. The outside children can have what is left. I never learned if my husband had any outside children, but it would not surprise me to learn that he did.

Saving for a House

I began to save for a house with my own money. He and I did discuss purchasing a home, but pornography, womanizing, and quitting his jobs made it difficult. I believed that if we had a home and we broke up, there would be equity to be divided between us. If he left me with the house, mortgages were not as high so I could manage with a little extra work. These were my thoughts based on the character of the man to whom I was married. He was still attending College at nights to become an accountant. Whenever he would stop working, the financial load was all on me until he felt he should return to work. He said he was doing some accounting on the side, but I never saw much of that money.

Purchasing a House

It became my job to find a house within our budget. However, no matter where I found one, we could afford, he refused to let us purchase it. I found houses in Brentwood, Long Island, Cherry Hill, New Jersey, and Moorestown, New Jersey that he did not like. This was in the seventies and prices of these houses were very good. I investigated purchasing a fixer-upper Brown Stone in Brooklyn he said no. No matter where I found a house he was not satisfied. Most of the money for the down payment I saved directly from joining a savings club called a Partnah. After slavery was abolished the slave owners agreed to sell their land to their former slaves before returning to their native country. Partnah is a system that was developed by the slaves to accumulate the purchase price for the land on which they slaved for generations. Partnah/Partner – This is an agreement formed between a specific group of people to put a specific amount into a pool each week. Every week someone from the group gets to 'draw' the total amount from what was pooled together. The number of people in the pool determines the number of weeks the pool lasts before a new cycle begins. Every person has to get a draw. In a

Partnah it is very important that the person who is the banker is someone of impeccable reputation and responsible character in the community.

Trapped into Moving

He came home one weekend and wanted us to look at homes Upstate New York. Public transportation was not affordable back and forth from where I worked. I went with him because we were going as a family and just to see houses for comparison. When we got there, the salesman greeted him as if they knew each other. Then to my shock and horror I learned my husband went to an open house without me and placed a non-refundable deposit on a three-bedroom two-bathroom townhouse. When I asked why we could not get our $3,000 back they said he made a binding contract. We either had to move forward with the sale by purchasing the house or lose the money. I remember thinking this man has done IT again. Once we were home, he began to give me his usual vexing speeches about the joys of moving with him and being a stay at home Mom. He knew this was something I would have wanted, but I had given up on the dream because of his refusal to maintain stable employment.

Whenever he sensed that I was angry beyond words, he would go on a browbeating tirade to intimidate me into an agreement. This time we were going to be happy, both of us not just him. He was going to come straight home from work and was not going to quit his job anymore. I could not trust him to keep his word. His refusal to be accountable was a major bone of contention in our marriage. I knew he was lying as always, but I felt trapped in the marriage and I did not want to lose the money which I had saved. I was looking for a way out but found myself being pulled deeper into the web of lies and deceptions. I considered his taking our money to pay down on a house without my knowledge as a strategy to keep me from working. This would mean putting the well-being of myself and our sons in his hands. I was also becoming more assertive on my own behalf which did not settle well with him. It was not as easy to intimidate and make me cower as before. In addition, I had sole custody of his sister

Princess. She would need to be place elsewhere because she was a ward of the State. I could not move her outside the jurisdiction of New York City and take her with us. In my favor she was in her last year of high school and was about to graduate.

Princess Graduates

When I brought his sister Princess home to live with us she was a traumatized girl who had lost her mother, abused by her stepparents, and by some of their family. I taught her to value herself in all the ways that I had come to value myself and she had to follow my rules. I told her to wait until she was married to have children which she did. I did not want the possibility of her feeling she was less then because she did struggle with having what I considered a correct sense of her womanhood at that time. While she lived with us, I encouraged her to enter Miss Jamaica USA Beauty Pageant where she placed well. Princess graduated from high school with honors and went to college. She earned a two-year degree in Secretarial Science. After she graduated, she went to work for a large bank downtown where she is an Executive Assistant today. She later married and had two children in marriage.

Moving to Middletown

His stepmother took me aside while we were there to settle Princess in and asked me if I was sure I wanted to move with my husband. His stepmother and I would sometimes talk about the behaviors of his womanizing and she knew he was violent towards me because she witnessed an incident on a visit to their home. I explained to her that I made the decision to move in spite of what I knew about his behaviors because I wanted to give us this one last chance. She sighed! Then said good luck!

The Friday night before we moved, my mother had some of the sisters from her church come to her apartment to pray for us. My husband was invited but he did not to attend. I went and they prayed over me and my children. We finished packing up the U-Haul and moved Upstate in early July 1976. I had to resign my job. The commute, along with childcare expenses, cost more than I would be making. I settled in and unpacked while he went to work and came home late every night. His work schedule was an office 9-5, but he rarely made it home before midnight. He never came home one night straight from work even though he had made that promise. I knew his promises were just words without substance because he did not have the character to back them up. The children and I had dinner most nights alone except for an occasional Sunday meal with him.

Cultural Isolation

Moving to Middletown was not only isolation from my financial power, it was culturally isolating as well. I was a Jamaican woman in a world with very few people of color. I experienced the cultural isolation as being very painful because I did not see many people like myself. I felt that we were seen by some of our white neighbors as anomalies to be probed rather than individuals who were to be embraced as culturally different, yet every bit as valuable. While I had no dislike for white people, I was not accustomed to being among so many of them. I felt overwhelmed by their numbers and what I felt were their probing questions. I had a sense of cultural belongingness in Jamaica because of the levels of sameness in my culture that I was not experiencing among so many whites in America. Living among so many whites left me wondering what it would feel like to have their sense of belongingness as a Jamaican woman in America. Absolute legitimacy comes from the fact that God loves us. However, having the sense of legitimacy is a very important intangible asset that we all need to provide for each other. My neighbors were particularly focus on what my life was like growing up in Jamaica. I felt a deep need to keep the shameful secrets of my painful past buried and hidden from their view. I did not want my shame disturbed and felt it was my business. Besides, I could not see how their knowing about my past would be of worth or value to me or to them.

Douglas's First Year of School

I attended an open house for Douglas alone because he was not available to accompany us. I would have liked it if we were there as a family, but that was not possible. The boys and I rode with our next-door neighbor and her husband. Whenever anyone asked about my husband, I lied to cover the shame I felt not knowing where he was and wondering what he was doing. I shared that he was working very hard to provide for us. I met Douglas's first grader teacher who appeared to be a competent and caring older woman. I liked the way her classroom was decorated, and I had a general good feeling about her. My son was going to be one of the only two children of color in her classroom.

However, many of the families including myself had concerns that were voiced, but not heard. We kept hearing that there was a KKK member on the school board. When the parents met with the principal, he assured us that it was only a rumor, but those of us who were people of color left the meeting feeling unsettled about the issue. When one of our African American neighbors ran for the school board later that year, she and her family received threatening phone calls that were racial in language. She lost the election and the family eventually had to move away. I shared the rumors and concerns I had with my husband.

Finding Employment

I made attempts to find employment, but the closest shopping center was thirty minutes away by car. I thought I could work as a clerk, or a checker in one of the stores and bring in additional income to help meet the needs. That would require him to come straight home from work and watch the children. However, when I mentioned this to him, he simply said, no! Watching our children was woman's work and that is why I was home.

Another Broken Promise

In the middle of our financial struggles, my husband came home one evening and said he was laid off from work. I knew that meant he had quit his job again because he was tired of working. When he finished his explanations, I said to him; "let me see if I am understanding all this. Your family will have no money since you quit you position at work because you are tired of working. We are currently behind in our mortgage and you just quit your job today. "What about us? What are we going to live on? A few weeks later we ran completely out of food, the lights were cut-off, and the water was due to be shut-off. The morning that the lights were to be turned off, he took the final cut-off notice to pay the bill that day. An employee from the lighting company came and shut off the light about 11 am the same day.

I told the worker my husband paid the bill this morning hoping I could buy time to call him. He told me no ma'am he did not. When I called, he told me he paid the electric bill earlier. I told him I called, and they told me if you paid the bill, you are to give me the number on the receipt and they will send someone out to turn the lights back on within an hour. My husband put the phone down and began to curse me out. He was aware that I could hear him. He wanted me to hear him tell those around him how much trouble I was. I waited refusing to hang up. "Do you feel better now that you have stabbed me? You knew the lights would be turned off because I could not get another extension." "I did not have the money to pay the bill." Then why are you telling me you paid the bill when you did not?"

Feed the Kids

I got some candles out and called my friend Samantha and asked her if she had any cooked hamburger. She told me to come over, so the boys and I walked to her house. I told the boys we were having dinner at Miss Samantha's and made it like a fun evening. When he came home that evening, he was angry. "Vivienne, why did you call me today about the light bill?" "You are my husband who else should I have called? It is impossible for me to get a job because of where you purchased this house." He did not respond to my comment he only wanted to know if I left him any dinner. "No! I asked Samantha to feed the boys this evening I did not feel right asking her to feed my husband." "His response was, Vivienne what do you want me to do?" My response was "I want you to at least keep a job and provide for your family."

You promised you would not quit your job. You were going to be the provider and come home from work on time so we could have some family time. If you got home earlier, I could find a part-time job to help us out. That is when I heard the most devastating words yet from my husband: "A promise is nothing but a comfort to a fool and you are the fool who fell for it." You are so right my husband! I am the fool who moved with you in spite of knowing that you were not looking out for me or our children's best interest. This was our last chance to get it right and you've squandered it away in your drive to dominate me."

He told me I was getting too big for myself. I don't know who you think you are Vivienne? Let me remind you who I am, we took vows together for better or for worse. You have made it your number one priority to see that I always have the worse. I have done everything you asked including the killing of our baby to keep this marriage. I wished I had told you to take a short walk off that long pier and raise my children without you." Vivienne, there you go again, always bringing that up as if it was against the law." Listen, I said this country made taking the life of an unborn child legal. If you really believe we have no consequences for killing our baby; you are a bigger fool than I thought you to be. He began to make a fist, but he seemed unable to move and I felt it wise to stop talking. I felt the pain and tears of us dying but I refused to let him see me cry and call me weak.

Lack of Resources

My friend Samantha who helped us out with food dropped by the house one morning to say hello. When she asked how I was doing I told her. I had no milk, no money to buy milk and did not know what I was going to feed my children for lunch or dinner. Samantha gave me a number to call for emergency food. When I called the number, they said I could come now, and she drove me there. They were helpful and I made an appointment to return for additional help. In addition to helping us with food they helped me get our utilities turned back on. I felt a lot of shame accepting help when he should have been working and providing for our family. Whenever I asked him about going back to work there was a violent argument. His limited financial support was short lived, and his lies were intolerable. I asked myself, Vivienne how much more of this are you going to take.

Final Straw

When we moved, I hid the credit card since I had no income to pay the bills and he made it clear he was not responsible for the credit card bills. I had forgotten to change our address when we moved so the bills went to the old address. One day I received a call from my mother telling me that the credit card company was calling her about overdue credit card bills. She wanted to know why I was using the credit card when I was not working. I told her I paid it all off before I left work and had not used it in over a year. I took the information she had for contacting company but before I contacted them, I went to my hiding place and the credit card was missing.

When I contacted the credit card company, I learned the bill was over $150. I requested that the card be cancelled without informing my husband. About ten days later he took a "hairy bank, out to dinner. When he attempted to use my credit card for payment, it was declined, and she had to pay for dinner. He came home quite chagrinned and I acted as if I did not know what he was talking about. The woman in question was someone that I knew. She had a husband and they both knew they were married. I felt no pain for either of them. He was embarrassed. Big woo. Here we were his wife and children living at the expense of the government while he attempted to wine and dine other women at his wife's expense.

Overtly Suicidal

Suicidal thoughts were a relentless companion of mine since I was seven years old. As I became an adult, I knew that suicide was a permanent solution to life's temporary situations. Yet, wanting to commit suicide was a constant thought that was second nature to me. As my life became increasing difficult, my depression increased the stronger my feeling of wanting to escape life through death. While Douglas was at school in the second grade and I was watching Graham play in the backyard one morning when I began to contemplate suicide with a plan that would end my misery. As I was deep in the thoughts of planning my death, I heard my son Graham calling Mommy, Mommy. As I looked up from the stupor of my despair, he had climbed higher on the swing set in the back yard than usual and needed my help to get down. So, I went and got him. Graham's cry brought me back to reality. It suddenly became clear to me that if I took my life my children would have no mother to care for them.

Chapter Nine

Separation and Divorce

My first attempt to leave him put my life in very real physical danger. I had been packing slowly in small amounts so as not to alert him, but he came home early one night and caught me packing dishes in our bedroom. When he saw that I was packing he threatened, "I will beat you in your face until you are so ugly no man will want you." I had to promise I would not leave. Ok. I lied. Although I had a plan, I needed money and the funds I had tucked away were in a bank in Manhattan. One day when the kids were out of school Samantha asked me to accompany her into New York City. I agreed to go with her, and we took our children with us.

Before we purchased the house and moved, I felt it was wise and prudent to save as much as possible in secret. I also put some of my income tax refund in that account. I withdrew what I felt would be sufficient for leaving. While I was there, I went to a nearby branch where we had a joint account to see how much of our money was still there. That is when I learned that our joint account was emptied out and closed. Over a period, he withdrew our money without my knowledge. I kept quiet to Samantha when she asked me if everything was alright after I left our bank. When I learned that he had emptied out our account I stopped feeling guilty for saving secretly and hiding my income tax refund under my maiden name. My husband felt he had me in a binding choke hold where I would find no exit. I had no job, no money, very little support, and no transportation.

Running Away

Whenever a Jamaican woman leaves her husband it is said she ran away and left him. At the time that I was leaving our mortgage on the house was three months behind, but he still was not trying to find a job. The day after my trip to the city, I contacted my mother to ask if I could come back home temporarily. My mother asks me why and I told her I just needed to leave because I could no longer live with my husband's cruelties. She said okay! My mother said to me "I knew something was wrong, but I wondered when you were going to tell me." My mother seemed compassionate towards me which was a new and strange experience between us. My mother said I could sleep on the couch and the boys could share the extra bed in my brother's room. However, I would need to make financial contribution towards the household expenses and be responsible to feed me and the boys. I said okay! It was an extremely humbling experience to go back home to my mother who warned me not to marry the man that I married.

Final Plans

During the time that I was making plans I was very careful not to upset him. One night he came home ready to beat me down because I cussed out one of his "bits" on the side over the phone. I knew of his many adulterous relationships throughout most of our marriage. While he was not the husband or father I desired, he was still married, and I took issue with this woman calling our house. We were living in Upstate New York, she was in the Bronx, and he gave her the unlisted phone number to where his wife and children lived. When I asked her who she was and the reason she was calling my husband, she immediately became defensive. She was another Jamaican woman. "I don't have to tell you why I am calling him. He may be married to you, but you are wife in name only from what he tells me." "Well, I may be a wife in name only, but I'm still his wife and you are only one of his hairy banks, one of his many bits on the side. Stop attempting to glamorize the fact that you are in a wrong relationship and with a married man. Get off my telephone and do not call my home ever again. If you want him that badly I can arrange to have him packaged and sent to you postage paid." Then I hung up!

Truth Comes Out

The "hairy bank" who called me gave him her chapter and verse of our encounter on the phone when he saw her before coming home that night. By the time he got home he was stirred up and ready to spew his rage at me like a boiling volcano. I was terrified, but I was feeling a lot of rage towards him myself for giving this woman our home phone number and so many other issues between us. He asked me, "Just who do you think you are telling off my customer?" "Oh! She is a customer! Is that what you are calling your "harry banks" these days?" He rushed towards me and I threw a cleaver at him which was the first thing I saw, and I was sorry at the time that I missed him. I knew it was time that I left his sorry carcass. When I threw the cleaver at him it went whizzing by his head, so he backed off. With him it always took extreme measures for him to back down until he revamped his predatory intrigue on a deeper level against me.

The children were upstairs in their bedroom, and I don't know if they heard the commotion that night. I never underestimated his judicious need for revenge because he always had a comeback that would grab me by the throat. After we were married, and he adopted Douglas, but he did not want him to know he was not his biological father. I reluctantly agreed not to tell him the truth then because I wondered how it would affect my son when the truth came out. At the time I told him that I would tell Douglas the truth when I felt he was old enough to know. Well later that night when he had his comeback in place; he told me as he was leaving the house, that upon his return the following day he would be telling Douglas he was not his real father. The following day was Friday and I was planning to leave that Saturday, but I delayed the plans. I was on such an emotional overload I could not process it all that quickly. I could not sleep that night after he left the house. I do not know where he went and honestly did not care. As I thought about the issue of him wanting to the keep it a secret that he was not Douglas's biological father I realized he had set me up just in case. I decided that when my son got home from school that Friday evening, I would need to be the one to tell him the truth. He was just a seven-years-old-boy at the time.

I concluded that it was going to be damaging and create trust issues between me and my son no matter who told him the truth about his real father. This was an emotional land mine and I knew better than to think he was kidding. I sat my seven-year-old down and told him I had two things to tell him: (1) that his Dad and I were going to be separated and (2) that my husband is not your real father but your stepfather who adopted you. He began to cry, and I felt my son's heart breaking at my betrayal and wondered if trust would ever be restored. He asked me who his real father was, and I told him his name. Then he asked me where his real father was and I did not know, so I lied and said he was dead. I cried buckets behind my lie that night.

I should have just said I didn't know where his father was, which I did later. When I told Douglas later that I did not tell him the truth about his father, he said, "Mommy I know you did not tell me the truth." My shame in being unmarried, pregnant, and abandoned by his father was still having a very devastating impact upon me and I still felt the deep loss of belongingness and legitimacy. When he come home on Saturday night and told me he was going upstairs to tell Douglas the "good news" about who his real father was, I said, "it's too late he already knows." He was so deflated that I wished I could have taken a picture of him. He was left with nowhere to go with his sense of entitlement to hurt me. I knew that when it came to my husband, revenge was always just around the corner. I barricaded myself in the boys' room that night and did not come out until he left the next morning.

Plans to Leave Resumed

I continued to put the pieces of my plan in place to leave without his knowledge. Besides my mother the only other person I took into my confidence was Samantha. I felt as if I was walking a tight rope of terror that could explode at any moment. I looked in the local Penny Saver Paper and found a handyman that would move the furniture to my friend's basement. I contacted him and we negotiated a price. I told him I would call him on the Saturday morning when I was leaving telling him what time to come. I also investigated renting a car. I had a learner permit from paying someone to teach me how to drive when I took control of my own salary. However, he refused to drive me to take the test for my license and the driving teacher wanted more money than I could afford to pay him to take me. I was stuck temporarily until I decided to ask my friend Samantha to rent a car in her name for me. To my surprise she said yes. I called the car rental company back and reserved a car in her name to be picked up that Saturday morning. Now everything was in place. My mother was expecting me on any Saturday that I felt it was safe to leave.

Leaving Saturday Morning

For me leaving the marriage was not the best thing to do; it became the only thing that I could do to escape the brutalities of our relationship. I was not asking him to be perfect, but his hostile attitude and his violence against me was pandemic on all fronts. He would constantly tell me you just need to suffer more. Today I know that whenever anyone speaks like that, they are in a demonic partnership with the ancient enemy of God against who God says that I am. After he left that Saturday morning, I waited for a half an hour to begin implementing my plans. While I was speaking with the handyman on the phone, I saw him driving into our driveway and told the handyman I would call him back later.

When I inquired why he came back he said he had a feeling I was not going to be home when he came back that night. I was stunned, but I had to think quickly. So, I said, if you think that I am leaving you, why don't you stay home today. He stood there and studied me for a good five minutes then said, I don't think so. Where could you go? You can't go back to your mother's house. I kept silent and smiled until he got back into the car and left. I remember thinking after he left, you are so arrogant in your wrongdoing that it has left you thinking I have no way out so you can keep doing whatever you want to do.

I made the phone calls again and my plans to leave were back in action. The handyman came, packed up my furniture on his pickup truck and took the furniture to my friend's house. My friend Samantha came with the station wagon and helped me put all the clothes and what I had packed especially my pots, pans, silverware into the station wagon. By the time I was finished moving out of the house it was almost noon. Before I left the house, I took of my wedding band and placed it on the kitchen counter with a note. We drove to Samantha's house and my furniture was packed in her basement. I paid the handyman and we drove to the Bronx. I took the back roads for two reasons. One I was terrified of running into him in the process of my getaway. Two I was driving on a legal driver permit, but I did not have my driver's license as yet. I was scared I would be stopped by a state trooper, so I drove in the right lane like the traumatized battered woman that I was.

When I thought the boys could not see me, I would pull the car over to the side of the road and vomit. I don't know why I was vomiting but I just did. I only stopped for bathroom breaks and food for the boys, I could not eat. When I got to the Bronx it was late and I was an exhausted wreck. I bathed the boys, fed them what my mother had prepared and put them to sleep in my brother's room. I then set out to finish unpacking the wagon. I then took a shower and made a bed on my mother's couch. It was just after midnight when the phone rang, and I knew it was him. The phone was in my mother's bedroom, but I could hear every word he was screaming. "Vivienne ran away and left me. She took everything, all the furniture and she ran away and left me. I bought her a house and she ran away and left me." He bought me a house! We bought a house. In all of his screaming I never heard him once say, she took our children then ran away and left me!

What I Saw

I understood that after we were married his reason to exist was to dominate and control me. His loving me and caring for me was not on his radar even before we got married, but I could not see that because I felt so undeserving at that time. I only saw that I was damaged goods and here was a man who wanted me? My sense of being damaged ran much deeper than being pregnant the first time without a husband. It was the incest and molestation of my father; being abused by my father's family, being abandoned by my mother because she felt she could not care for me economically without my father. The deliberate neglect of my father and his refusal to educate or protect me from other predators like himself. Being abandoned when I was pregnant. All of these issues and more left me feeling as if I was the inherent shame who belonged to no one not even to myself. This shame ran so deep within the core of my unconscious being it made all of my decision for me. The man that I married was aware of my need to have a sense of belongingness, worth, and value by being attached to him.

Returning Upstate

I drove back to Middletown on Sunday morning and my friend returned the rented car and drove me back to the Bronx. I was free, but I still did not feel free from him. Knowing his character, I felt my life was still in danger because there is no reasoning with those who have been getting away with abusing you. Once I was back in the Bronx, I set about getting Douglas into school and I began to search for a job and daycare for Graham. On my way to seeking employment that week I ran into someone that I knew. One of the secretaries in the agency where I worked for the proposal writer. She mentioned to me that one of the junior secretaries resigned and there was an opening in the secretarial pool. I took the train to 125th Street and went up to the personnel office. Some of the people I knew still worked there. I applied for the position, but I needed to take a typing test. It had been about eighteen months since I saw a typewriter. I was given an hour to practice and when I tested, I came out at fifty-five words per minute and I only needed to type fifty, so I was rehired. Life was looking up, but I was still very fearful whenever I would leave the house for any reason.

My Husband's Rampage

After I left, he went on a rampage! He called everyone we knew and gave them his rendition of how he was such a good and faithful husband and provider to me, but I took all his possessions and ran away. All my friends who had my mother's phone number began to call her reporting on the scandalous things he was saying about me. I became very fearful and went to speak to someone about domestic violence issues. I was even more afraid when told I was in more danger away from him because I left. I developed a routine of getting Douglas to school, Graham to daycare and myself to work. I felt like a prisoner. If I did not have to go somewhere, I stayed home. When I went out, I always went with another family member when one was available.

An old friend whom I had not seen in years contacted my mother to ask how I was. My mother handed me the phone, as she began to speak, I knew she was calling on his behalf and I hung up on her. Less than thirty minutes later he was on my mother's phone again cursing my mother out. One minute he was telling my mother he wanted me back, and the next he was calling me bad names. I took the phone out of my mother's hand and hung it up. Predators look very innocent, but they can change posture to impress and manipulate the person who will assist them in dominating their prey. He was excellent when it came to wear the disguises that would give him the advantage against me.

Domestic Violence Continued

One evening following our separation he came to my mother's apartment. When he said who he was I asked my mother not to open the door. She said, "Vivienne, he is your husband, besides you have family here he won't hurt you in front of us." Before I could respond she opened the door. He walked past my mother, grabbed me around my throat and body slammed me into the wall in front of her. In my family, divorce is not an everyday occurrence. We make every effort to reconcile marriages, but reconciliation requires a two-way dialogue of mutual change which he and I were never able to achieve because his way was the only right way. With his hands around my throat I was struggling both to breathe and get his hands from around my neck. When my teenage brother came out of his room, released me. He was asked to leave, or the police would be called so he left.

Sunday Morning Visit

Several weeks later a Sunday morning while my Mom was at church, he came to visit his children or so he told my brother. My family felt that the boys needed to see him. In addition, he promised he came with peace and not animosity. He was using the children as leverage to see me and this never worked well. For as soon as he said hello to the boys, he then needed to talk with me alone. It was very important that he speak with me. I asked my brother to take the boys into his room. I had come to always expect an eruption of at least verbal violence with him. I wanted to shield the children, however, it never worked because we would escalate so quickly. His mask of quiet demeanor could erupt on a dime. The more important it was for him to win the argument, the more relentless he was at using all the cunning strategies in his arsenal. He lived on the premise of, I will and must win all arguments at all cost against my opponent. I as his wife and the mother of our children was his primary enemy.

So, I agreed to talk with him in the living room. I invited him to sit but he refused. So out of fear of being hit physically or by a barrage of his verbal attacks, I stood as well. His question to me was: "Vivienne what is the three (3) things I need to do to get my wife and family back?"

"Well, why do you want your family back after everything that has happened between us?" Now in his mind he wanted his family back because he was entitled to having his family back. Marriage and family for him was on his terms and it did not matter to him what I wanted, needed or how his behaviors were affecting me and the children.

A few days before this Sunday morning visit, he invited me and the children out for dinner at a fancy restaurant near where we used to live. When he invited us out, I asked him, why so fancy when I could not get you to come home? His reply was flat, "I just wanted of do something nice for my family." The boys wanted to go because he made the offer in front of them. After dinner he wanted to know if I wanted to go back home to Middletown with him. I said no! He told Douglas at another time that if I came back to him, we could move back to our house and have a better life. I wanted to scream at how he was trying to manipulate me by using my seven-year-old-son.

The Saturday before his last visit to my mother's house, his stepmother called to say she had a conversation him. "He told her he was going to do all in his power to get you back, but after he gets you back, you are going to be under "Heavier Manners" than before." In Jamaican language, he was going to make me pay because I had no right to leave him no matter what he did. I also learned that the reason he took all of us out to dinner was part of his plan to bring me back home. My heart was no longer in the marriage or into him. Therefore, it was pointless for him to try but he was not able to see that. I thought about his question then asked him again: "You want to know the three things I need from you in order for our family to be restored." "Yes" came his reply.

Reconciliation List

Knowing that he would not agree to do any of these things, I thought to myself, Vivienne: What have you got to lose by giving him the list he is asking for?

- I want you to stop physically, mentally, and financially abusing me.
- I want you to stop sexually abusing me with pornography, womanizing, and STI.
- I want the total and complete removal of all pornographic materials from our home.
- I want to be able to work and have control over my own money.
- I want you to maintain continuous employment so we can have a good life.
- I want a marriage where my voice is heard and respected.

I also wanted to know where he found the money to pay the $900.00 on our three months overdue mortgage in less than a week after I left. Where did you get the money to pay the overdue mortgage since we were getting assistance to feed our children and you were not working? I had grown so weary with him and his deceit, yet I really did want to know where the money came from. For me these were just normal expectations for a man who wanted his family back. For him however, I had no right to any of these expectations. I was just supposed to take him back, but I did not want him back. I fully understood that these orders on many levels were too tall for him. I was no longer willing to attempt any compromise with him until or unless he put forth massive efforts towards change. The cost of compromise was too high for me because it would continue to be a one-way street.

Final Breaking Point

His face was in total disbelief when he heard my list of demands. He said, you expect me to do any or all of that. I said YES! These are my expectations for us to be restored. Like the flash of a light bulb, his hostility went from zero to one thousand. He accused me of calling him a "BOY" and disrespecting him. I was backing away from him, but he kept coming toward me. He slapped me across my face with the back of his hand and I fell on the floor. When I fell on the floor, I quickly began rolling out of the way to keep him from stomping me. As I jumped up from the floor, I felt something break inside me.

I picked up the first thing that I saw and hit out of fear that he would hurt me worse and to slow him down. He faces began to bleed and his rage increased. My face was burning, my head was throbbing where he had slapped me, and my lip was bleeding. My siblings heard the commotion and came into my mother's living room and pulled us apart. When my siblings broke us apart, he turned to look at the boys before he left and said, do you see how your mother is abusing me. She cut my face and I am bleeding. He was still making attempts to fight me when my brother told him, leave you are not welcomed back here.

When I went to see my counselor that week, I told her of the incident and asked her to help me get a divorce. She gave me a referral to a branch of the agency that handled divorces for a very small fee. I made the call the next day for an appointment and the process would be in motion as soon as I could pay the filing fees. I also went to court and was granted an order of protection against him. When I left my husband, I had no intentions of going back to him, but I felt we would just live apart while married so that I would not need to struggle with the issues of being a divorced woman. His attitude of hostility, aggression, and rage made up my mind for me to divorce him that day.

House in Foreclosure

Shortly after the fight in my mother's living room I received a call from the bank that held our mortgage saying the house was now in foreclosure. The real estate agent he hired to handle the rental agreement also contacted me. She asked me to get the house out of foreclosure because the tenants were paying rent to him, but he was not paying the mortgage. While he paid the three months after I left with the boys he stopped paying when he began to collect the rent of $500. I told her that unless we could come to an agreement that gave me control of the rent, I would do nothing. She said that they could not do that because they had signed a lease with my husband. Well, call him was my response. I knew that if I had gotten involved without some assurances I would be stuck with the responsibility while he collected the rent.

I spoke with a lawyer who recommended that we have legal papers drawn up for him to sign over the house to me. I would be responsible to collect the rent and pay the mortgage until the house was sold. Upon the sale of the house he would then have the contributions that we both made returned to us. The lawyer contacted him, and he agreed to come to his office and sign the documents turning it over to me until we could sell the property. This would have given us both some financial benefits if he cooperated with the process. The appointments were made for four different occasions, but he did not show. After four missed appointments the lawyer said Vivienne, cut your financial losses as you have your personal losses and move on. I returned the money that I borrowed, and we lost our house. The loss of our investment as Jamaicans was a hard blow for me because I invested when I knew the risk of losing it all was very high. To him buying a house under deceitful conditions was a means of power and control over his wife.

Divorced

When I returned to see my divorce lawyer, I told her we lost our home so there would be no property settlement. I asked for custody of our sons Douglas and Graham and child support. I requested that she get me legally free along with my children from his tyranny under New York Laws. I did not see the point of listing all our filthy laundry for public consumption. It took over three months to serve him with the divorce papers because he kept evading the process servers which I hired. I finally had to meet the process server across from the building where he lived early one morning and point him out. I wore flat shoes and as soon as I saw him coming from his building, I said there he is, and ran down the steps of the subway and got on the train. The conductor closed the train door and I was out of harm's way from him. I stuck my tongue out at him. LOL! No, that was not mature, but it felt good at the time.

Temporary Move

After the second incident at my mother's house I felt that I needed to move out on my own. I was not angry with my family because I had put them in the middle of a messy situation. I also believed that since I was the one who married this person, they should not be expected to handle it anymore. His hostility and rage were fixated against me, but he was quite charming and personable like my father was. His charm is what he used to disarm anyone before he moved in to take out who he considered prey. I applied for a section eight apartment and was approved, but there was a waiting list. My godfather rented me a one-bedroom apartment in one of his buildings while I waited for section eight. I put the boys in the bedroom on a pullout bed and slept on the box spring in the living room. Life was simple and basic, and the boys and I made the most of it.

One night he came by the one-bedroom apartment late after 10 pm at night. Somehow, he found out where I was living and came to my apartment banging loudly on the door to be let in. When I refused, he became noisier and began to attack my character saying I did not want to let him in because I was hiding a man. That was not true! I had an order of protection from another incident at work. After he cussed out my boss I was told if I did not get the order of protection I would be fired. I filed a copy of the Order of Protection with the local Precinct. When he refused to leave, I called them, but I was told just don't open the door. The neighbors called but no matter who called, the police never came. I was barricaded in the apartment with the boys until he left the following morning. I called a neighbor asking her to pass by my door to visit her friend then go back to her house and call me if he was not there. Which she graciously did. After she let me know he was gone I left the apartment to go about my day

My Own Place

When my name came up on the section eight list, we moved to a two-bedroom high-rise apartment in the High Bridge Section of the Bronx in 1980. The boys had their own room. The apartment also had a long terrace on which I put a grill and a plastic kid's pool for the boys in the summer. I got a U-Haul and some help and drove back to upstate and moved my furniture back to the City. We cooked hamburgers, hot dogs, roasted corn on the cob on the terrace as our makeshift backyard during the summer. We settled in and the boys were attending school while I worked and attended school. I became very sick and passed out on the side of my bed one morning. When I went to the emergency room, I was told I had walking pneumonia.

The doctor told me I was very sick, but I explained I needed to care for my sons. A social worker came to see me and said I could get temporary foster care while I was hospitalized. When she told me, she would be right back, I took the IV out of my arm and left. Douglas was out of foster care and I had kept him out. I did not want to open that Pandora's Box in my life again. I called my sister Rachel and she came over and cooked several meals so that the boys and I could eat. My brother Paul came and cleaned the apartment and did some necessary laundry.

It was at the end of this struggle that the divorce papers came in the mail. There was no settlement. All I had was my freedom from being abused, well in theory. I was told that a copy was sent to him so I was concerned he might just show up unannounced to voice his disagreement over my divorcing him. I was granted a divorce and full custody of our sons on October 5th, 1979. The night I got the divorce papers was a bittersweet night for me. I thought to myself, never have I given so much and received so little in return. Although he retained a lawyer his lawyer only represented him in court once. He would not pay his lawyer to represent him in court, so his lawyer resigned, and the things ran their natural course. I was told that I had to go to Family Court for child support which I did but I had difficulty getting child support. He was ordered to pay $100 each month for both children. He came to Family Court armed with receipts of bills he paid, and I knew he did not, but could not prove it. So, I got what he had left from his salary after his needs were met.

Don't Let Your Father In

This order should not have to be given to Douglas and Graham. However, I was placed in that position because of his continued violence against me after we were separated and divorced. Our sons were caught in the crossfires between me and their father on many occasions. His visits with the boys was sporadic at best. I wanted him to see his children, but I did not want or need to see him because our interactions were hostile and violent. I felt a great deal of contempt for him! When it became clear to him, I would not come back to him the children became the pawn he used to cause me more hurts. This put them in a middle of our conflict, and they did not belong there. However, I was never able to find any way to keep him from attacking me in their presence and I was through "grinning and bearing any more of his abuses."

They were little boys and they forgot my orders when he showed up because they had not seen him for months and opened to door for him. The boys were in their pajamas when I came out of the bathroom. He asked if he could put them to bed and I hesitantly said yes. After he put them to bed, he walked out into the hall of my apartment and pulled out his copy of our divorce decree and began to wave it about. The boys did not know the divorce was final yet. I looked at him and said please leave. He began to make his way to the door, but as I opened the door to let him out, he grabbed my arm and body slammed me into the concrete wall. When my head hit the concrete wall, I thought he had cracked my skull open this time.

The commotion brought Douglas and Graham back into the hallway looking at their parents. He had me pinned to the wall and I hardly had the strength to fight because I was still physically weakened from my battle with walking pneumonia. I told Douglas to take Graham and go back into the room, but he did not move. Douglas spoke and said Daddy stop hurting my Mom. This broke his rage and he released me and walked out the door. I just dissolved into tears on the floor, the boys came, and we held and comforted each other. When I asked Douglas why didn't you go to your room with Graham? Douglas said Mom my feet couldn't move; they just couldn't move. I cried all night. I forgave my sons for answering the door they are NOT to blame for this or any other attack or quarrel between me and their father. Attacking the mother of your children is a sure sign that you are not yet a man. I received child support only intermittently. At times I was afraid to go to court and keep perusing the issue because I was always afraid that it would lead to a violent attack against me.

CHAPTER TEN

AN EDUCATED WOMAN OF THE JOHNSON CLAN

Following my return to work in Harlem late in 1978, I had a very good boss who was fair, strong, and he did not display any predatory tendencies towards me or anyone else. He was an African American man. His attitude was firm, and he expected me to work in excellence. This made our work environment very comfortable and I worked hard. If my work, home or church environment is predatory it causes me a great deal of stress and I do not perform at my best. I just survive rather than thrive in toxic environments.

Do You Want to Go to College? NO!

My boss Mr. Farham, who was the Deputy Comptroller of the agency where I worked, called me into his office one afternoon. I took my steno pad and pencil preparing to take a letter or a memo. When I sat down, he asked me if I wanted to go to college. Without any hesitation, I said, NO! I cannot go to college I'm not smart enough. He got angry and asked me the question again and told me that he wanted a different answer. So, I said yes, I would love to go to college, but I cannot go because I do not have my GED. While I said yes to him inwardly, I thought Vivienne how are you going to accomplish this? As stated earlier I took my GED after attending night classes in America but failed the exam by eleven points in the late 1960's.

Mr. Farham told me about a program at Turo College where I could attend college and earn my GED after twenty-four credits. He told me to take the afternoon off and go sign up downtown. If you do not sign up for college, you are fired! I do not know if Mr. Farham was serious about his threat to fire me if I did not register for college, fortunately I never had the opportunity to find out because I did enroll in college. My job was the only means to provide for my children.

Going to College

On my way downtown on the "D" train I kept saying to myself, Vivienne, who are you fooling? When you get there, they will tell you to get out and denounce you for the fool and fraud that you are to think that it will be that easy to go to college without a GED or a high school diploma. So, when I arrived, I told the Jewish woman registering students who sent me, and she gave me forms to fill out. I completed all the first set of forms that she gave me. Then she asked me if I was a high school graduate or if I had a GED. I said NO! Then waited to be humiliated. However, she said, you will need to fill out these additional forms and when you have completed twenty-four college credits with at least a "C" average come back to me. I will send this paperwork with your transcript and your money order to New York State Department of Higher Education (NYSDHE) in Albany and they will send you your diploma. I filled out all the forms.

I then filled out financial aid forms and again, I thought two sons, no child support. Vivienne run now while you can. I was terrified, but I did not run, I believe my feet refused to move. I stood there filled out the paperwork and applied for grants and loans. While I was there filling out the required paperwork, I thought about my father and my grandmother's refusal to educate me in Montego Bay. I thought about Aunt Rona saying I should go and be a hairdresser because I was too old to become formally educated. I thought about my father and Elsa who could but did not assist me when I first came to this country. I just kept filling out every form that they placed in front of me in shear desperation and hope. When I had completed all the paperwork,

I heard the registrar say, Mrs. Anderson, you are now enrolled in college and you may now officially register for classes. I was so stunned my tears began to flow.

I felt numb and kept pinching myself to make sure that I could feel myself, but there was something else that I also felt. I felt as if I was alive in a band new way for the first time since I went to Mt Alvernia High School in Jamaica on that interview with Gammie, but I was denied. I signed up for three classes each would be four credits. I needed twelve credits to be considered a full-time student and qualify for grants which I did not have to repay. The grants alone did not cover my tuition or books, so I needed student loans to complete my financial package.

The woman who was registering me for classes told me that I needed to take, English Composition 1, Accounting 1, and a Psychology Course titled, Self-Actualization. I wondered what in the world it meant to become a self-actualized Jamaican woman. I did not dare ask because I did not want to look and sounds like I was ignorant. I knew I was intelligent, but I did not know how smart I was. I wanted to be a business major because I felt that I needed to make money to support my sons, so being self-actualized seemed to be a tad frivolous, but I thought that I might learn something about myself and I did.

Only in America

Looking back at the course work it was self-exploration into who I was and could become which has been a tremendous help to me over the years. Many of us in my generation become teachers but in my mother's generation most of my aunts had some type of business venture of their own to help them survive financially, even when their husbands were good providers. Only one of my mother's sibling was formally educated in England as a nurse. When it was all over, I was enrolled in college and registered for classes, I was in shock! How could this be, no high school diploma, no GED, no money and I was enrolled in college to become a formally educated Jamaican woman of the Johnson Clan. Only in American I thought to myself could this be possible.

The Jamaica that I left as a young girl in my teens, it would have taken more than my willingness to become educated to make it happen. I was pinching myself all the way uptown where I lived with Douglas and Graham in the High Bridge Section of the Bronx. My mother's apartment was not far from mine and I had to pick the boys up from aftercare. I went to my mother's apartment and told her to sit down I had some news to tell her. I told her what happened early in the day and that I was now enrolled in college. I was a college student after all. However, after I finished telling her my story. I said to her "I am afraid I'm not smart enough to finish college."

Mom I'm Going to College

My mother said to me, I am going to pray for you every day so that you will come through and graduate. Then she said: "My child is going to college Thank you Lord Jesus." In 2003 all of her children went to visit her in Jamaica after she retired from being a Nurse's Aide in America, and an Ordained Pastor. She built a home from scratch on property that my grandfather left his descendants. She shared that she would pray every day and ask God to educate her children and grandchildren; that all her grandchildren will serve the true God, and not become joined to any types of cults, false religious practices or traditions.

I Got My GED

After two years of attending Turo College, I got my twenty-four college credits. I discovered I was smart after all and a good student. I had a passion for reading and studying was not difficult. So, I went back to the same lady and gave her the money order along with my transcript she sent them off to Albany, New York. A short time later I received my GED Diploma. I was so proud of myself the day that I received it in the mail!

Pass It On

When I shared my opportunity to get my GED at Turo one of my sister Sharon she also became a student at Turo College. When she acquired the twenty-four college credits and received her

GED, she transferred to Bronx Community College and became an LPN nurse. I took my GED with my "B plus" average and applied to Fordham University, Rose Hill Campus. I was accepted there and went on to graduate with a BA in 18th Century Social History. I did not have the educational background nor the support services necessary to support my skills deficit to handle a business curriculum. An African American Guidance Counselor at Fordham helped me to understand that in college, study what you love. I loved history and majored in Eighteenth Century Social history. I became self-actualized by studying what I loved as opposed to studying what would make money. Money is very important; it answers all things, but it must not be the primary motivation for who we become or for what we do. Someone once told me Vivienne build value in the lives of those you serve, and God will add an abundance of wealth to your life and the lives of your descendants.

Turo was a steppingstone to get the education God wanted me to have and I am grateful to Him for His intervention. I am also grateful to Turo College for opening their hearts to me and for being part of my journey to becoming an educated Jamaican woman of the Johnson Clan. I became the first person in my family to graduate with a BA from Fordham University Bronx, New York and the second to get a master's degree in America from Stetson University in Deland Florida. Thanks, Turo. Mr. Farham thank you for seeing the potential in me that I had long since abandoned in the pain of my childhood. Blessings to you and your descendants one thousand-fold. How awesome is our God who would intervene on the behalf of someone who was in too much pain to see His hand of intervention throughout the whole of her life. It took me five and a half years to graduate from college. I had no social life during those years, except for an occasional dance during semester break. My life consisted of work, school in the evenings, studying, taking care of my sons, and being in class on Saturdays and Sundays sometimes. I would take my boys to class on days when their school was closed, and they were very well behaved.

CHAPTER ELEVEN

FORDHAM STRUGGLES

During my Fordham years I was only able to work part-time during the school year. I needed to see to my sons' education and keep them out of trouble and alive. I and many other mothers' were always afraid our sons and daughters might get hurt; this was not about them being difficult children. The Bronx was a rough neighborhood in those days, and it did all it could to claim our children towards the dark side of life. While in high school Douglas was offered money if he would deliver drugs for someone, I am grateful that he had the courage to say no and swim against the current that drew so many of our sons and daughters into its web. While I did not consider myself to be a poor woman, I was raising my sons on a shoestring budget especially during the days of my becoming educated. This means that we lacked some of the necessities that I could not afford to provide for my sons. They were not the most popular kids, but they were very hard-working sons with good manners, and made excellent academic achievement which was my primary focus and wish for them. I was and am very proud of them both. I have been very blessed with my sons.

The one thing I did not want was for the words their father spoke in his anger against them over me divorcing him. He told me that I was too weak and spineless to raise our sons without them becoming juvenile delinquents. I said to him, you are making that statement because I refused to take any more of your abuses. "I will see you eat those words!" When you are a struggling single black mother safeguarding the life of your children, especially your sons, it feels like playing a game of Russian roulette.

He Missed Christmas Again

For their father missing Christmas was not an unusual event, but this one took the prize. In 1982 while I was a student at Fordham, he contacted us and asked the boys what they wanted for Christmas. The call surprised me because I usually had to track him down and he would still not show up. The boys got all excited and after saying what they wanted, they asked him what he wanted from them for Christmas and he told them that he wanted a silk tie. Well, he only wanted a silk tie! Here I was supporting our two boys without child support and he wanted "a silk tie." I was hot and fit to be tied at the nerve of him! I held it in and told the boys as calmly as I could, they could pick out a nice tie from their allowance and I would chip in a few dollars.

The boys asked if he could have breakfast with them when he came. While I felt it was too much, I agreed to make a special breakfast. In the back of my mind I knew that his promises meant nothing because he made them to see how much pain he could inflict on me. I said nothing to them about the possibility that he might not come and prayed he would keep his word to them since he was the one to initiate the occasion. I tried to make Christmas morning special by sleeping on the sofa in the living room or the boys would raid the Christmas tree before 6 am. My rule was we do not open Christmas gifts until 6 am on Christmas morning, but they could open one gift on Christmas Eve night which was usually not their first choice.

Our Own Christmas Tradition

Each year we would go down to the Bronx Terminal Market the day before Christmas Eve and buy a live Christmas tree for about $20.00. Only the really big trees would be left by then. We used to borrow a saw from my neighbor and cut the tree down at the bottom so that it could stand up in our apartment. I would use the branches to make a wreath for the front door. The boys and

I would decorate our tree with tinsel, garland and with pictures they drew from the time that they were young. In Jamaica we did not have a Santa Claus because we had Father Christmas the British equivalent and there was never a Christmas tree as I was growing up in our houses until I came to America in the 1960's.

On that Christmas Day Douglas and Graham were very excited about Christmas with their Dad. The boys even called him a few days before Christmas to make sure that he was still coming, and he assured them that he would be there. So, we went out and they picked out a tie for him. Well, they were disappointed when their Dad did not show up as promised on Christmas Day. He was not there to exchange gifts with them as he had promised. The fact that he called them and made the offer left them with a sense of assurance that he would be there. I began calling him after he did not show up at 8 am but he did not answer his phone. Instead of going out as planned I made dinner at home. When I called my friends and told them what happened they understood why we were not coming. My sons hardly ate any of their favorite foods that I prepared.

I was angry that once again he made loftily promises to his children which he knew he would not keep. For to him, "A PROMISE WAS NOTHING BUT A COMFORT TO A FOOL."

My Visit to His Job

The day after Christmas I told the boys that I needed to run an errand downtown. I was sufficiently angry with his behaviors to go and confront him. I got dressed and took the subway downtown to where he worked. I went to the receptionist and told her that my name is Vivienne and I told her who I wanted to speak with in a calm and friendly manner. Making a scene was not on my agenda. I felt that it was enough that I was there. I decided that going to his job to quietly confront him was my safest and best way of handling the situation. I also knew he would be too concerned with his reputation at work to behave badly towards me in front of people who saw him as a gentleman.

When he saw me, I could see the shock on his face. It was delicious! This gave me the courage to carry out my assignment.

I asked him if we could speak privately. I told him off about his evil wicked behaviors towards our sons and how much he ruined their Christmas. Once again, I said you made promises you did not intend to keep in order to cause me pain. What about their pain? To you a promise is "nothing but a comfort to a fool." Our sons love you unconditionally and believed you and once again you broke their hearts and ruined their Christmas Holiday. They missed out on having fun with their friends because of you. How could you be so mean and hateful to our sons? "I promise you if you do not come and make it right with them, I will be back. Just before I turned to leave, I gave him the tie the boys bought him for Christmas.

He Came Under Threat

The boys were unaware of my visit to him as I did not want them to be further disappointed should he not show up again. However, they were sufficiently angry with him that they refused to go to the movies with him to see Gandhi. He wanted to take them to see Gandhi. When he said he would take them to see the movie Gandhi. "I ask him to please take them to see something they will enjoy. Allow them to choose a movie that they want to see. You treated them horribly on Christmas Day and they did not ask you for your promise." I thought that ET would have been a better choice and directly made that suggestion. When he came was wearing the tie the boys picked out for him. Offering to take them to see Gandhi was his way to sabotage spending time with our sons. He came to see them under my threat, but he did not bring the gifts the boys asked for. On his way to see them he picked up a couple of "stales" after Christmas sale gifts the boys never opened. While he did come and wore the tie, they got him it still fell short, but I give him credit for coming.

Financial Struggles

During my first year of college I was laid off from the agency in Harlem, budgets cuts. I applied for unemployment and Medicaid to cover the boys medical. I went to section eight and they lowered my rent to fit my salary decrease. However, the boys were attending catholic schools which required books and dress clothing. Having done all of this I had the essentials covered, but my education was now at risk. I was in dire financial straits and after careful consideration decided to ask my father for his help. This was difficult because I left when I was pregnant with Douglas and saw very little of them. My relationship with them continued to be turbulent because they just could not let my past go. Yet I was expected to forgive them and forget their past behaviors against me while they refused to leave any of mine in the past. They still only wanted a one-sided relationship of my total loyalty, and an impervious compliance for the behaviors they wanted from me while they were abusive in my opinion. So, I stayed away. I was tired of the hostage taking one sided relationship that I had endured all my life.

My Father's Help

However, I was playing for what I considered very high stakes, my education. I contacted my father after completing my first semester to say I was in college. However, with my lay off I was hard pressed, so I swallowed my pride and asked for his help. When he came to the phone, I told him that I needed some financial assistance to finish school and I was only in my first year. I further explained that had I been given the opportunity that I was seeking to get educated back in Jamaica and when I first came to the United States, I would be finish with my education by this time if support had been in place for me. I could feel my father squirming under the weight of my words, but I was undaunted. He wanted to know if their father was supporting our children financially and I said he was not unless I agreed to be physically satisfying with him. My father asked me what kinds of assistance I would need. "Well, I said I have two growing boys and food goes quickly and for school I needed $500 each semester for tuition, plus books, and travel expenses until I graduated. I also told him both boys were in catholic school, but I had that covered."

I also told him I worked two full time jobs in the summer, but I still needed help with the boys. I told him the story of how their father took Graham to help me out but he came back in two days with scratch marks from his girlfriend's dog. He told me he would think about it and get back to me and let me know what he could do. I thanked him and said I love you. I did love my father, but I also hated my father concurrently. My father called me back a week later and said he would help in the following ways. He would help me with books and the $500 extra towards tuition at Fordham University each semester. He would buy my books each semester and he would help with food. There was only one catch, I had to come to Queens every other week for the extra food and money for books at the times they were needed. I had to come when Elsa was not there because she would not approve of him helping me. He also offered to sponsor the boys for a couple of trips to Jamaica during the summer by paying their air fare. I agreed to his terms. This time my father kept his word until I graduated from college.

Summers in Jamaica

When the boys spent summers in Jamaica my Aunt Inez was the natural choice to keep them. My cousin Stephen would take them on outings, and they went to all of the Seventh Day Adventist church functions. This included daily morning and evening devotions at home. While they were in Jamaica for the summer one year, there was a Coup attempt against the Administration which placed the country in a crisis. Aunt Inez who was keeping the boys called to say she was afraid because the opposition party was running night raids and people were being killed. She did not want my American born sons to be caught in a crossfire. I did not have the money to go immediately but when I called my father, he booked a redeye flight for me to go and bring them home.

Meltdown Days at Fordham

During my Fordham years I had a major meltdown one morning after I took my sons Douglas and Graham to school. I don't really know what triggered this meltdown but there it was. I took an overdose of sleeping pills in an attempt to commit suicide. Let me say that I did not always understand why my past was causing me to regress to childhood. Traumatic memories would come out of nowhere and engulf me so deeply that I would lock myself in a dark closet in a fetal position for hours fearful I would hurt myself if I came out of the closet. These were time when I would cut myself in places where no one noticed. When the boys came home from school, I had to resume my mother role and do the best normal possible for me.

Flashbacks and Accidents

Once on a visit to a psychiatrist, I told her that I was having what is now known to me as flashbacks from my childhood. I recalled the doctor telling me that the things that I experienced as a child were over and not happening in the present therefore, they could not be the cause of my having periodic meltdowns. She also told me that I was just having problems adjusting to life and I should basically grow my little self-up. I believed her since she was the expert, therefore, when these flashbacks continued to come out of nowhere and attack like a two-by-four I had nowhere to go. I could not and did not have any explanations and I was too afraid by then to tell anyone that I was experiencing these flashbacks. On two occasions in the Bronx I had flashbacks that were so terrifying and intrusive while I was driving that I hit a tree on the side of the road.

Suicide Attempts

One morning I was home and after the boys left for school, I began to feel like death was my only hope. So, I took a bottle of extra strength Tylenol along with some other sleeping pills. After I took the medication that morning I got into my bed and began to drift off into what I hoped would be permanent sleep. However, as I was drifting down this dark tunnel following a light as tiny as a pin head, I suddenly saw a window and my sons Douglas and Graham were trying to wake me up, but they could not. So, I began to struggle to wake myself up. In the process I fell off the bed. I think I must have knock phone off the nightstand and somehow the police were called. While I was on the phone, they were asking me a lot of questions to keep me talking. On some level I wanted them to let me die, while at the same time I wanted them to help me live for the sake of my sons.

The Police Came

However, when the two police officers got to my door, I was unable to get up off the floor and open the door to let them in. I felt parlayed lying on the floor from the medication that I had taken. So, they knocked on doors down the hall and found a neighbor. Biff, the super of the building let them into my apartment and they took me to the Emergency room where the doctors pumped my stomach. Having my stomach pumped was not fun at all, but it saved my life. After the doctors pumped my stomach, they gave me a prescription for more sleeping pills and sent me back home. (LOL) I barely knew this neighbor because I isolated myself from everyone. My sons were sociable, but I liked being alone. My neighbor and I became very great friend and her family adopted us as their own. My sons and I spend many of our holidays at their house for many years until we moved. We still keep in touch.

My neighbor Vera had a way of looking at life that helped me a lot during those years. She would say to me Vivienne you are going to die from legality of the brain sitting in your rocking chair on the front porch in Jamaica. Of course, I would remind her that in Jamaica we do not have porches we have verandahs. We would just laugh. Vera and I would take our food stamp every month and drive in our old, but reliable cars to College Point and buy groceries to keep our freezers full so that our children could eat during the month while we struggled through college as single mothers. We would also sit with our schedules together and sign up for classes to give each of us time off in case we had to see about each child. When one of us had to be in school the other looked after the children.

Religion Classes

While I was studying at Fordham University, it was mandatory to take religion classes which included reading the Gospels and the Old Testament. It was during those years that I can look back and see the hand of God as He used my love for reading to draw me close to Him. The passion I had for reading as a child gave me an exposure to World Religious thoughts, ideas and ways of looking at life that was different from what I knew. As I went through the process of become educated, I was also becoming more aware of the God who I knew existed. I found myself comparing what I heard on the occasions that I went to church with what I was hearing in my classes. This comparison and reading the Bible for myself, brought me back to seeking the God of compassion rather than a vengeful God of wrath and punishment.

Maybe God Is Real

I was totally oblivious to the fact that my spirit was reaching for the God that it knew was different from the one that my parents and Christian Leaders were modeling in my life. I kept thinking that I was on some intellectual pursuit to find something other than God since I already concluded that God just did not work. While God existed to me in an ethereal sense in the universe that He created; I did not consciously experience Him as real, tangible, or practical on an everyday level. I think God just laugh at my saying this. Oh, really Vivienne! God was wise in the way that He led me to Himself. He brought me to Himself all by Himself.

Today I find myself praying and loving my sons who have also dumped church because of the hurts and wounds that they have received from the churchified. Not to mention the hurts from their parents who were divorced and did not always behave well or like grown adults in their presence. God is in covenant with me for my children. Today I stand back and pray to God and trust in His love for my Douglas and my Graham. I know that like me, they will be back and find God for themselves because God is faithful to all my generations.

Fordham University Graduate

In 1984 after I graduated, I became an Elementary Teacher in the New York City School system. My mother was right proud of me and my father came to my graduation. Elsa made him take of his Tuxedo and dress in a regular suit without his tie to see me graduate from Fordham University. His chest was busting, and I thought that his heart was going to explode from pride. I do not recall any other time when my father showed any pride in me as his daughter or my accomplishments. Before that, he seemed to behave towards me as if he was cheated out of a male heir and I was not even second best. When I got my diploma my father practically snatched it from my hand to see my name next to the degree I had just earned.

The fact that he got all dressed up in formal wear to come and see his daughter graduate from college left me wondering if the comments that Mammie made about him not wanting to waste his money sending me to school was true. Given who they all were it is difficult to know what was true. My father took pictures and sent them to Aunt Rona in Jamaica to show her that I graduated from college which she said was impossible. He appeared to have taken the sides with those who pronounced me hopeless, yet he was standing front and center to see me achieve what he had been told and appeared to believe that I could not accomplish.

That fall Douglas was headed to high school and I wanted him to have a better chance than the public schools in my area of the Bronx appeared to be offering for his future. Once he passed the test for Catholic High school, we chose All Hollows as the catholic high school for him to attend. It was staffed by men of Dominican Priesthood which I hoped would provide him with positive responsible male influences in his life. The neighborhood thugs were making attempt to recruit young men including my son to engage in illegal activity. When Douglas was approached, he said no and came home and told me about it and I agreed with him that his decision was correct.

I needed to get additional educational credits to complete my teaching requirements and certification. At the time New York City was experiencing a teacher shortage so I enrolled in education classes at the College of New Rochelle satellite campus in the Bronx. While in class on the first Monday night another adult student came into the room. I knew that look on her face and I did not want her sitting beside me. Christian women gave me the creeps back in those days, because most of them seemed to be angry, aggressive, hostile, and bitter just like us unsaved women. Only the unsaved women treated me better than the so-called saved women did. I did not want to hear how wonderful and good your God was, and you are still hostile, mean and nasty. It just did not compute for me and Christian women frankly had no credibility because of their attitudes.

I did not want her sitting next to me, so of course, she sat right next to me in a crowded classroom. The professor asked us to exchange phone numbers, so we did. These were the days of land lines. I threw Mattie's number in the trash. I had no intentions of ever calling her for anything. I am not really sure why she called me, but she began to share her testimony with me about how she was a former Jazz singer who drank and did drugs but now she was saved and a pastor's wife. I would listen to be polite, but I thought what in the world do I care. I don't drink, I don't do drugs, I don't smoke, and I am not a Jazz Singer. My few visits to clubs was not all that because I felt so out of place there. Going out and getting drunk in order to have fun felt wrong inside myself. It was not a good fit for me. I went only occasionally as their designated driver and to shut up my friends who thought that I should get back into the dating scene and find a man. While they were very sure that a man would cure what was ailing me, I was equally sure that the distraction of a man along with their demands for my time would keep me from graduating college. My vices in those days were Yoga, writing poetry, and reading. Intellectual pursuit was a childhood survival strategy that I fully developed, and it worked to keep me from losing my mind. I used antidepressant and walking to numb the personal pain that I did not understand. I also did not know what I was supposed to do to heal from the pain of my spirit and my fragmented past.

I was a recluse as my few friends would call me back in those days; and I was quite content being solitary. I still am. I developed a comfort in being with myself and I got to know myself very well and I liked it that way. I did not have to put on a mask when I was with myself. I could just be me in whatever mood I happen to be in. I went places with my children and occasionally with friends but when there was no specific place to go, I was quite content being home with the boys cooking, baking, watching TV, or movies, or reading. It worked well for us especially since money was always in short supply. The boys had friends who came over and they went to their homes. We did well by my evaluations and with God's continuous unexpected interventions. One of our favorite places to visit was museums, with the Museum of Natural History being the most often visited by us because the yearly membership was not expensive. Mattie's continued to call me, and I felt bullied by her. One night when she told me on the phone, she felt that I needed to accept Christ as my savior I knew what that was and said yes to get her off my phone and off my case.

CHAPTER TWELVE

CRISES OF MY FAITH

That sinner's prayer was literally a fire insurance prayer for me and the boys. Although I did not like feeling bullied, I am grateful that Mattie's did not take my refusal of her witnessing about Jesus personally. I am grateful to God for sending her to a sinner who was lost. If she had not come who knows how differently the outcome of our lives might have been. My salvation is a miracle and God sending her to me in my classroom is part of that miracle. Mattie's personality was bold and strong about her faith. She was unashamed of sharing God's goodness and how He changed her life and she wanted me to experience that change. I went to church only for weddings, funerals, christenings and I would always leave early.

Moved to Queens

After I graduated from Fordham, my father encouraged me to move back to Queens so he could be close to his grandsons. I agreed to the move because Douglas was getting pressure from unwholesome forces in our Bronx neighborhood to deliver drugs for them. They offered him $800 but he kept saying no and I am grateful God gave him internal strength to keep saying no. Another incident came when I was in the park with the boys and I saw two men making a drug sale of what I later learned was cocaine. While my sons were great kids, excellent students, I was very concerned about the influences around them with no strong male figure in their personal lives. I thought my father's womanizing was past because he was in his sixties by then. I also hoped he wanted to be a good influence on his grandsons since he did not do well by me. So he helped me get a two bedroom in a private house in Queens. Soon after we moved, the landlady decided she did not want our dog Apollo in our apartment. We were threatened with having to move if we could not find a place for our dog. I had made it a point to tell the landlady that my son had a dog and she said that would be no problem. He was a good dog and she said yes then did an about face.

While we all loved the dog, it was Douglas's dog that he loved and took responsibility to train and care for. I made attempts to find a home for the dog, but we could not. When we called the humane society, they told us they would adopt him out, but put him to sleep in less than forty-eight hours after we dropped him off. Apollo was a beautiful German shepherd and Douglas had trained him very well. We were all heart broken and he was angry with me for moving. I remember thinking Jesus, can you please cut us some slack here! I moved my kids to get them away from the pressure of becoming drug dealers and we lost our family pet. In addition, South Ozone Park had changed and one evening when the boys were walking home from the library, there was a shootout in the street on Rockaway Boulevard. I felt that we should have stayed in the Bronx.

My Second Fire

The night of the fire was less than a week after Mattie's called me at home and we prayed the sinner's prayer. Jesus did cut us some slack on the night of the fire! We lived when we should have died, all of us! I fell asleep that night in the living room after we had dinner. They boys had a disagreement and Graham woke me to ask if he could sleep in my room. I said yes. Later that night I woke up smelling smoke, but I did not see a fire. I checked the stove in the kitchen, and it was turned off. Then Graham came out of my room saying, Mom, why is it so hot in your room? I do not know, I answered. When I attempted to turn the lights on, they were off. When I tried to use the telephone there was no dial tone. It was extremely hot in the apartment. I tried to get Douglas to wake up, but he had locked himself in their room and was not waking up. I ran downstairs in my flannel nightgown taking Graham with me. We knocked on the landlady's door. I told her I think there is a fire upstairs. I can't see any flames, but it is too hot upstairs. I told Graham no matter what happens do not come back upstairs.

When I went back upstairs, I tried to open the boy's bedroom door again, but I could not. I was in a cold panic and had an open vision of my beautiful son Douglas laid out in a casket. The son whom I had sacrificed so much to give him life. It terrified me. I began to scream his name, but he did not wake up. So, I stood on the stairs and prayed this desperate prayer: "God, I will go anywhere you want me to go, just please, please, please, don't let my son die." Douglas woke up and began screaming. I told him to open the door because the place is on fire and I could not open it. He did and the landlady's son helped get him outside. When I got downstairs the ambulance, police, and fire departments were there. I was exhausted and in shock. We were taken to a local hospital where the doctors told me the next morning that we all had so much smoke in our lungs, he did not know why we were still alive. In addition to the smoke we inhaled, Douglas had some burns on his face and hands, but the outer scars did heal. My hair had gotten singed and my hairline was scorched, and I have some sores until they healed. I remember thinking, Vivienne if you had died in the fire where would you have gone! It was very a sobering experience.

The ancient enemy of God was attempting to bury me and my entire lineage in a smoldering grave that night. But God! Who is rich in mercy! God, who is Sovereign, drew a line round about us. God said to His ancient enemy! NOT SO! NOT SO! NOT SO! This horrific experience brought on a realization that I needed more than my education to have a successful life. However, deep in the core of me I felt God, why didn't you let me die? This was not the first brush with death. I did not want my sons to die, they were innocent, but I was not. I had killed my baby to hold on to a marriage that was already in the graveyard. The fire left us devastated and I ended up back at my father and my stepmother's house. I really hated this because I was kicked out of their house when I was pregnant with Douglas. While we had a ceasefire; the deep feelings that were broken during the summer of 1969 and before were only slightly crusted over and we were never reconciled. It did not take much to stir up the old layers of pain that were buried alive from the traumas of that summer and of our preceding years together.

Tragic Mistakes

One of the tragic mistakes we make as human beings, is that we underestimate how alive and embedded our pain is and the negative power of never having gone through a healing process. I was taught the value of time healing all wounds without apology or reconciliation. This is a falsehood! We are usually clueless as to how easily our ancient wounds will explode in our faces when they are constantly being bumped by the ones who seared our hearts. When my father agreed to help me, I pretended that the hurts and abandonment of 1969 along with all of his childhood abuses were all better. When he asked me to move back to Queens, I felt he had done some good things like attending my graduation which allowed me to think that he had changed. While at my father's I began to search for an apartment. The boys and I needed to get back to having our own space so we could return to our family routine. However, that proved to be a difficult task because the prices on rental property had rapidly increased in a short time. The referrals that I received from the Red Cross were not places I wanted to take my children to live. Besides they were way over what my budget could handle.

The Cost of My Father's Help

In the process of my apartment search, my father came to me one day and told me he knew of a three-bedroom apartment for rent. I told him I only needed two bedrooms. He then went on to explain that he had a friend coming from England and she needed a place to stay when she came to the States. The friend could live with me and he would help with the rent so I would not have the whole expense by myself. It sounded too good to be true and I knew him well enough to know that if he was willing to put money up for rent on a regular basis there must be a catch somewhere. So, I listened and waited, and he just kept on saying how much of a benefit it would be for me if she lived with us. I asked him why you don't let her live in your house since we are leaving. No! He told me that would not work for my wife. Why? It just would not! He stated emphatically!

Crass Request from My Father

Now my father was a great help to us during my college years and I was grateful. So, he was now ready to collect payment for helping me. This friend of his coming from England, was one of his paramours. I was to house her because his wife would not suspect there was anything between them if she was staying with us. You could tell her that she was a longtime friend coming to the States. I could come and see her at your house without raising suspicion because I would be visiting with you and the boys. I recall asking him if he helped me to move to Queens because he knew she was coming. My father said I had a tricky mind for thinking that way. He went on to say, when he was visiting with her the boys and I could go see a movie and he would pay for it. I looked at my father and said, it would seem you have all this planned out for me, how kind of you.

Whil-e Elsa and I were never close, and I did not always like her, I was incensed at the arrogance of his insensitive request. I had to calm down and catch my breath. His suggestion got me so upset that I began to hyperventilate. I was a child conceived in my father's adultery and a wife who was abused by the adultery of my ex-husband. Now my own father wanted to involve me in his crime of adultery against his wife. I said "NO! NO! NO! I will not do that. "How can you asked me to do something like that Pops? What will I say to my sons about who this woman is that you will be coming to our home to see while you are married? How will I be able to tell my sons that this type of behavior is wrong when I am in partnership with you while you are committing adultery with someone who lives in our home? For me to do this, is to accept that my ex-husband was right in all his adultery and pornography against me and his sons." I knew he was a notorious womanizer; but to ask me to keep his "hairy bank", his "bit" on the side in my own home. This was too much loyalty for any father to expect from his daughter no matter what he has done for her in her adult years.

Predators only Want Your Compliance!

My refusing his request to have his mistress live in our home became a stumbling offense between me and my father. This time he ordered me and my children out of his house. Once again, my values on morality clashed with my fathers, but this time I was happy about it. In the first case, it was him wanting me to abort Douglas, now it was to allow his paramour to live with my family while he committed adultery with her in our home. It simply would not do! I decided I was moving to Florida to start over there. This time I did not tell Elsa what the issue between me and my father was. I felt that she should not hear about it from me. Ever!

Sexual Brokenness

Sexual brokenness and boundary violations rooted in immorality both my own and my parents ran pandemic and unchecked in my life and I felt that steps had to be taken to remove its hold from me and my sons. The breaking of generational consequences is not enough. The character traits that led to the immoral behaviors must also be changed or it will do you no good to break off the consequences. I was conceived in adultery and my father saw no issues with that. When it comes to sexual violation being conceived in an adulterous relationship carry a heavy load negative spiritual, emotional, social, and financial consequences. My father was angry that I as his daughter felt his behaviors of committing adultery was wrong at my conception. I told him in a conversation that he was wrong to be with my mother and conceive me when he was married to someone else. That it was his responsibility to keep his marriage bed pure. It takes two to have an uncorrupted marriage. He looked at me in anger and walked away. I unknowingly fell into the same trap and was awash with guilt, shame, and grief over it for many years. I had paid a very high price with my oldest son because although I did not know it at the time, he was conceived in adultery also. I wanted the boys to see that different choices had to be made for them to avoid the same traps. However, my father was blinded by his lusts and saw me as betraying him by not signing onto his scheme to house his "bit on the side."

Leaving Saturday

That Saturday morning as the boys and I was packing to leave and go stay with my mother until the school year ended. My father was still angry, and Elsa was very upset that I was being asked to leave with two children. She felt I should stay, work an extra job over the summer and save so that we could move. I was working part-time on the weekends as a hostess in one of the airlines first class lounges as well as teaching full-time Monday to Friday. As Douglas and Graham were taking our few belongings from the ruins of the fire to the new car, I purchased to take us down south, my father began to berate me in front them. Douglas stepped up and said: "Grandpa, please do not speak to my Mom like that. It's not right." My father continued "the reason that you could not maintain your marriage is because of your uptight morality on sexual matters and your hate for pornography." I shot back "yes" I hated my husband's pornography and womanizing, and I hate your womanizing. The only difference I can see between you and him is that you are very much older but not yet wiser." Suddenly the deep well of my vaulted pain began to overflow the borders of its hiding place.

Explosion at My Father

Suddenly I began to say, "I recall when I was a little girl that you would pull my dress over my head and beat me with the leather raw-hide belt that you kept soaking in an empty five pound butter pan of water. You would beat me until I urinated on myself because you would not stop beating me until I stopped crying. Imagine, you are beating me with a water soaked raw-hide belt and I am not supposed to cry. I would hold the screams in my throat to get you to stop hitting me which lead to me urinating on your precious bed. Then you would beat me more for wetting your bed while you were beating me. You used to hit me on the top of my head with your knuckles until is dissolved into the floor whenever I made a mistake or forgot to do something."

My father's face turned pasty grey and he appeared to be hyperventilating as I released these accusations against him. "You refused to educate me when I was growing up. You molested me! Then you and Ina, your live-in-woman abused me when we all lived in Trench Town and you tolerated her cruelty towards me. Any woman in your life could tell you anything about me and you supported them. You did not believe me when I told you of the things Grammie your mother did to me. The only woman you opposed concerning me was my mother." Elsa was in shock looking at me as if I should not have said any of it. I do not know why these memories surfaced at that time because they were not in my conscious thoughts. These events were painfully buried alive and surfaced because my father could not find his stop button when it came to him abusing me. When that come out, my father's face began to contort with indignation. Secrets that I never shared with anyone took a quantum leap out of my vault and his reaction turned violent towards me on a dime. The next thing I knew my father rushed to hit me and my seventeen-year-old son Douglas was on his way to defend me against his grandpa's violence.

Elsa and I stepped in between the two of them and I grabbed and held Douglas so that there would not be a physical fight with my father. While I felt that my father was completely out of line and deserved a good thrashing, I could not conceive of Douglas giving it to him. This did not seem right to me in spite of my father's pernicious behaviors towards us. The feelings of anger between Douglas and my father were mutual. I constantly had to back my father off my son while we were staying in their home temporarily. We clashed one day when he wanted to tell me what to fix for my sons breakfast. I explained to him that I was grateful to him for giving us a place to stay, but will you please allow me to feed my children what I know they will eat for breakfast.

I knew he had a hostile attitude towards me and Douglas because no matter what he did as a parent or as a man he considered himself to be right. This was the fundamental issue with him, he was relentless in his power drive for domination over others. If he could not dominate me for his personal gain, he wanted to destroy me as prey. My father like my former husband could not be reasoned with! My father was in his sixties and still behaving like an adolescent boy in heat. He became angry because he expected everyone to be under his spell of supremacy or he would spare no expense in destroying you.

I had asked my father not to scold my children while we were there, but he felt that was a wrong request. My father would bring all varieties of petty complaints to me about Douglas. I would remind him that he is only a seventeen-year-old boy, so stop expecting him to act an adult. His expectations of Douglas were just as ungodly as the ones he projected onto me as a child. I told my father one day stop picking on my son because you wanted me to abort him. When this confrontation with my father at his house was over, we finished packing our car and finally got on the road to my Mom's house. Douglas never liked my father even before he knew that he wanted me to abort him.

While we were on our way, my father called my mother to complain that I was a very ungrateful daughter. For even though he helped me when I was in college, then took me in with my children following the fire, I would not do one small favor for him. While he told her that he took me in he did not tell her that while I was there, saving to move I paid him rent, and bought food for me and my children. He did take us in, but it was not a free ride nor was I expecting one given who he was. If I borrowed his car after my Rambler died, I had to replace the gas that I used for my trips. He commented the first time I borrowed his car, my car dose not run on water. I told my father; I already replaced the gas in your car that I used for my trip. When I told my mother what really caused the argument between us was him asking me to keep his "bit on the side" in my home. Her mouth fell open, and she said. "He is still like that, "yes" I replied, "He is still like that."

I stayed with my mother for about a month this time and after the school year ended, we were on the road to Atlanta to check Douglas into Morehouse College. Then Graham and I would go on to Florida to begin our new life. I felt New York did not hold anything promising for me and I needed to find a place where life could be successful.

Chapter Thirteen

Florida, Here We Come

My decision to move to Florida was considered risky by the standards of my sons and other family members. Douglas was going to college in Atlanta on a full academic scholarship at Morehouse College, while Graham would be entering the 8th grade in Florida. My sons liked living in New York, the "Big Apple", but there was so little left from the fire and starting over in New York was too overwhelming a task at the time. What was not burnt up was so waterlogged and filled with smoke that I wanted to puke just being in the same room with the remains of the fire.

Starting Over Again

We were alive and that was enough to start over somewhere else. However, while the sights of New York were miles away, the smoldering embers of living from crisis to crisis were never far away. My family felt that I was having an emotional meltdown and they were right, but that happened later. I still had a child to get through high school and two sons to get through college. Before I moved to Florida, I felt it was wise to inform the father of my sons that I was taking our children out of state to live. While we were still at my father's house, he had taken it upon himself to call and tell him we were burnt out. He only informed me of this on the day that my ex-husband was coming to visit. He was pleased that I had fallen on hard times. I sat looking at him and smiling knowing he was relishing what he considered my downfall. He offered no help at all to us after the fire which is why my father contacted him.

Moving to Florida

I seized the opportunity that day to let him know we would be moving to Florida. With my father sitting next to me I would not get any lip from him. I also told him that if he wanted the boys to come to New York and visit him, he would need to pay all the travel expense. Since we had no visitation arrangement and he was not paying child support I felt he should pay their way to New York and back to Florida. He only asked that I provide him with a telephone number when I was settled, and I agreed to do so.

Douglas Graduates High School

When Douglas was graduating from All Hollows High School, he called his Dad to tell him. The graduation was being held at St. Patrick's Cathedral on 5th Avenue in New York. He was there with bells and whistles to take pictures of Douglas' graduation. During their years of attending catholic schools, he paid one semester tuition for the each of the boys. After his picture taking, he left and went on his way. His picture taking of Douglas was for bragging rights where he put forth very minimal effort. Graham was also an honor student. He never offered to take the boys out to celebrate their academic achievements. A friend of his told me later how proud he was that his son had a full academic scholarship to Morehouse College and his other son was an honor student. I was miffed that he was there to enjoy the curtain call of mine and the boy's hard work. After the graduation ceremonies, I drove the boys, my sister Sharon and my niece Aisha to City Island, New York where went to one of the outdoor restaurants by the water. We shared the cheapest meal I could afford. We celebrated my firstborn graduating from high school in America and going to Morehouse College on a full academic scholarship.

My son Douglas was the first child born in America in our family. He was first to graduate high school and head to college on an academic scholarship. I was right proud of him and of us as Jamaican immigrants achieving so much in-spite of all we had endured. I would tell the boys I am not raising an uneducated black man so do well in school because you can. "Do you hear me?" Douglas says I was a drill sergeant about curfew and other issues and that he sometimes did not like me very much. However, today he is a man who is a responsible father, and one who works hard and cares well for his family. I made mistakes, but I did something right.

Extra Money

While I was planning to move to Florida, I made attempts to secure employment, but no one called me for an interview. One day after school year ended, I received a check for $2,300 from Child Support Enforcement. I was also paid my July teacher's salary at the end of June. My August salary would be sent to me after school opened in September. The check covered some of what he owed me, and I was grateful it came when it did. That is all the money we had which included travel, food, gas, and hotel expenses on our way there. I gave some of the money to Douglas and left him in Atlanta, hoping for a miracle because we needed one. It is not that I felt or even believed that I deserved a miracle from God considering the abortion, I was hoping against hope for the three of us.

New Friends, New Hope

The night before we moved to Florida my mother's friend contacted a friend of hers in Ocala, Florida. Connie asked her friend and her husband to look out for us because we were moving there alone. She also had us to speak with each other on the phone. Lady Duran said it was fine with her for Connie to give me their phone number and to contact her when we got to Florida. On my way to Florida we stopped in Atlanta and completed the process of enrolling Douglas into Morehouse College. I was worried about him because of so many traumatic events throughout his young life including almost dying in the fire. Yet, he held on and graduated from high school with a full academic scholarship and honors. I was impressed with Douglas and Graham for their academic achievements given how difficult our lives were. The night before I moved to Florida, my mother and her friend Connie prayed for me and the boys. My mother and her friend asked God to watch over us and to give us favor with God and man. God answered!

Arrival in Florida

Graham and I drove from Atlanta to Florida and I contacted my mother's friends as soon as we got there. The Duran's were very kind, caring, and friendly people and I was glad Connie suggested the contact. We still keep in touch today. In Florida my newfound friends helped us to rent a condo with a Tennis Court, walking trails, and swimming pool for $300 per month plus two months security. I purchased some used furniture to see us through until I was working again. Nothing fancy two beds with mattress and box springs. The man at the thrift store gave us the bed frames. I also purchased an outdoor beat-up wicker set with ugly yellow and green cushions for the living room, and two chest-of-drawers. My new friends gave us a black and white TV, and a dining table with three chairs. We were set and I packed all of the pots, pans, dishes, and silverware that we salvaged from the fire and carried them with me.

I was always able to find employment easily and would take whatever job I got until I could do better. I told my mother that I was going to Florida because it was warm there and I felt frozen inside. I needed to thaw out from the hard, cold parched, scorched landscape that New York had on me and my family. Not to mention the utter disaster of my life in- spite of all my hard work. After we settled in, I went to the School Board in Ocala, Florida and registered Graham for his last year in junior high school. I also registered with them for a position as an Elementary Teacher and for subbing while I set about preparing for and taking the Florida exam to become certified as a teacher there.

Make Do Jobs

While I was waiting and anxiously checking with the school board weekly, I took odd jobs such as house cleaning, factory work, and working as a home health aide to bring money in for food, rent, and gas to travel, car payment, car insurance and other expenses. These jobs paid minimum wage which was $3.35 an hour in 1987 but some income was coming in. The Red Cross gave us $300.00 after the fire in New York that I used get work clothes and other vital necessities that we desperately needed after the fire. I had three suits to my name and a couple of skirts that I sewed by hand. My mother sent me to learn sewing skills in Jamaica when I first came back to her. I had a few blouses, pants, and jeans that I got from the Red Cross in New York. We washed our clothes very often to be clean whenever we left the house.

Going for Prayer

When Lady Duran invited us to church that first Sunday in Ocala, Florida I said yes. My son Graham asked me when we got home Mom why did you say yes to going to church since we do not go to church. I told him because they were very kind to us, we should repay their kindness and attend church on Sunday just one time. Lady Duran asked me to come early to be a part of praise and worship service. Of course, I made sure that I was late for the praise and worship service. I was only going to show my appreciation for their kindness. God had other ideas. Although I was forty-five minutes late the praise and worship were still going strong; when I arrived and sat towards the back of the church with Graham for a quick getaway when the preacher would begin winding down to call people forward.

Well, Pastor Davidson called the people forward before he preached that Sunday morning. This was highly irregular because I attended church on and off where the altar service always came at the end after the preaching. So, I stood in the pews feeling a strong tug within my heart to go to up for prayer but, of course, I was not going. I was there for a one time visit only and would not be returning. The more I stood the stronger the tug on my heart became, until I got an idea. Let me go and ask for prayer to find employment to care for Graham and myself. So, I told Graham I was going for prayer to find employment. As I was walking, I felt like crying but I kept my tears from flowing.

I Got Good and Saved

There were five pastors on staff at that church and they all came down and began to minister to the congregation. Many people were there for prayer that morning. I kept feeling that I was there for a reason other than employment. I was not accustomed to being in churches where the pastors made specific efforts to minister to the people before they preached them under shame, guilt, and condemnation. When Pastor Davidson came and stood in front of me, he looked into my eyes and spoke I felt a shift inside of me. When he asked me: "Won't you ask Jesus Christ into your heart today? The dam inside me broke and I began to weep, yes! He led me through the sinner's prayer, and I accepted Christ as my savior that morning for real this time. After I prayed the sinner's prayer, he and other pastors laid their hands on me and prayed a long prayer. That was the first time that anyone ever laid hands on me and prayed for me. I totally forgot the reason I gave myself to go up for prayer. That Sunday morning, I got good and saved.

I Knew the Difference

I instantly knew that something was different in me after I prayed the sinner's prayer that morning. I felt the pure, calm, peaceful presence of Jesus Christ inside of me that day. Never before had I ever experience such a feeling in any service, it was so amazing! God used a man whose heart was pure to bring me into His pure river of healing and cleansing love. Today, I know that when my father and his mother buried me alive it was to realign my spiritual DNA for satanic purposes. While I had a lot of wounding by the time, I was seven years old, I was never able to return to myself until that morning in First Assembly of God in Ocala, Florida. Prior to that Sunday morning I felt like I had an alternate self. After church we went home, ate lunch, and then went back to the evening service. From that day forward becoming a follower of Jesus Christ became my new passion.

Lifestyle Changes

Whatever lifestyle we are engaged in before we accept Jesus Christ becomes our identity. When we leave or give up that lifestyle for Christ, we must replace it very quickly with one that is of greater significance and healthier or we will become a vacuum that is capable of housing anything. Nature abhors a vacuum and the ancient enemy of God will quickly fill the empty space with something more deadly than what was there before. Listening to jazz, reading and writing poetry was fun, but it left me feeling empty and hollow inside. There was something always missing from my life and I did not really believe that God could fill that space, but He has. I was searching for a God that was not distant and disconnected from me and the issues of my life. Prior to that day there was a deep dark hole that nothing I tried could satisfy. I made a conscious decision that trying to fill this deep dark hole inside my soul would never happen, so I would just have to live in that state of internal emptiness.

When I made the decision to move to Florida, it appeared irrational for me to move to a state where I knew no one. I really did not have any consciousness of why, I just decided I am moving to Florida. Ocala, Florida was very different from New York and we experienced quite a lot of culture shock, but we adjusted. We quickly embraced our life in Florida because I was searching for a way out of the chaos that was our life. In time, I developed an understanding that the witchcraft/obeah practices of my father and his mother opened the door for the satanic forces of hell to pursue me to bring me and my lineage into what they had spoken over me that night they buried me alive in the woods. The blood of Jesus Christ supersedes all other blood oaths, blood covenants, and generational demonic devices. The blood of the Lamb trumps all the darkness from me and my lineage to a thousand of my generations' biological seeds.

Living in Florida

We moved to Ocala in early July and it was now October. I told Graham in mid-October that we were almost out of money and I did not know how we were going to pay the rent, car payment, and light or phone bills in November. He asked me: Mom what you are going to do? I told him that I was trusting God to help me find work soon, but if I did not find work, I would sell the used furniture take the money and return to New York. He was not happy about that solution because he was beginning to make friends at church, school, enrolled in football, and participating in the youth ministry activities, as well as doing well in school. While Douglas played basketball in high school, Graham played football and was a wrestler they both did well in sports. Leaving was the only alternative I could see if I did not find work that was bringing in money on a regular basis. I checked with child support in New York, but there was no movement on the case. Many people have asked me why I didn't go on welfare. I don't know, I did not think of going on welfare again.

Still Unemployed

The day after Graham and I talked about our financial situation I received a call to be a substitute teacher at an elementary school for one week. My first day there I went to the principal's office during lunch and spoke with him. He told me they were expecting an opening in the third grade where I was certified. Ocala, Florida was one of the fastest growing cities in America and the third-grade classes were over-crowded. He would need to open up another third-grade class to accommodate their growing school population. They were waiting for a trailer to be delivered that would house the extra third grade class. "Would you mind being in a trailer all day?" The principal asked me. "No, not at all!" I never saw a trailer until I went down south. How bad could it be I thought? I would be working. I let him know I took my test and received a temporary certificate to teach elementary school in Florida.

He took my information and told me he would call me when everything was ready. I kept substituting teaching. I had offers for Sunday jobs, but I did not want to take Sunday's off because going to church was helping me to cope. The only difficulty with being a substitute teacher is that subs got paid monthly rather than bi-weekly as regular teachers. However, the benefit of this was, it would be a larger sum of money because I worked for an entire week plus several days. So, we would continue to roll with the punches, tithe and meet November expenses. On Saturdays I cleaned two houses. I was now beginning to be hopeful and shared this with Graham. He was excited he would not have to move back to New York in mid-semester.

Ocala, Florida

On the morning of October 29th, 1987, the principal called to let me know that the third-grade class was formed. The trailer was delivered on time and all the furniture was in place. Would you be able to begin work in the classroom on October 30, 1987?" I said yes sir. I made a special meal and Graham and I celebrated that we could stay and have greater stability. The problems of living under the stronghold of the spirit of chaos and destruction is that life was unstable no matter what I tried to do. I began work on that Thursday and testified at church that following Wednesday night for the first time about how God provided a teaching position so we could stay in Ocala, Florida.

Everyone was happy but surprised to hear that we were having financial difficulties. I only shared my issues with Lady Duran, and she kept my confidence. First Assembly of God was a congregation that was over ninety percent white at the time and opened their arms to me and my sons. I was more welcomed there than I have been in churches that are ninety percent people of color. When something happened, it was handled. When discipline was needed it was done and the individual was quickly restored to full fellowship and not left sitting outside the camp. First Assembly of God was a relationally driven faith community and I developed great and lasting relationships there with people who are still a part of my life today. My Heavenly Father used this precious church body to begin restoring some of the necessary good things that we were missing as a family.

Graham made friends and had a healthy social life with other young people there. When Douglas dropped out of Morehouse College and came home to Ocala to live with us, he was embraced as well.

Voices in the Night

One of the issues that was a tormenting problem before and when I became born again was the issue of having the abortion while I was married. The torment of the abortion never really left me. There was a constant daily reminder as I would sit at our dining table with my sons to have our meals and feel the loss of the third child that should be there. My acceptance of Christ brought with it a new heightened sense of our wrongdoing. While I was forgiven for the iniquity of having an abortion; there were consequences that I needed to work through. My mind needed to be renewed and I needed to see our "choice" from a divine perspective rather than the intellectual rationalization based on the legality of abortion and our appetites to embrace a culture of comfort.

Being an adult when I entered college to become an educated woman shifted my intellectual patterns of thinking. This was a good thing, yet, there were aspects of my old thinking process before my education that were rooted in pain, abandonment, and rejection on all levels. I began to accept as fact that abortion was not as bad, and I once thought it was. However, when we begin to come into agreement with our predators, we have developed toxic "fear bonds" with them through their mind-numbing manipulations. When I was having an intellectual conversation with others who supported the pro-choice position, I never told them about my abortion. As long as I maintained a position of intellectual interpretation concerning our "choice" to abort; I could pretend all was well until I tried to fall asleep at nights. Whenever a piece of my emotions concerning the abortion broke away, it was like an emotional train wreck jumping my intellectual tracks. I could hear the tormenting cries of my baby at nights when I tried to sleep. Once when I told my ex-husband I was hearing her cries in the night told me I was losing my grip on reality. I told him no, I am not, she is crying out to me, but I am helpless to do anything to stop her from crying. These were a tormenting spirit that felt all too real to me at nights.

At First Assembly we were greatly encouraged to develop a daily routine of Bible reading, prayer and meditation. Later my counselor suggested that I added journaling which was very beneficial in my healing process. Cultivating a relationship with God through Christ was bearing fruits of stability for us, but it took my children sometime to accept that the changes were real. Life in Christ began to bring me into greater levels of strength internally and externally. My turmoil's did not instantly leave, but they began to become more manageable as I chased after the God of the Word. I also began to learn to accept that God really did love me. The one thing that continued to torment me and kept me awake at night was hearing what I thought to be my baby's crying out in pain of the abortion process. The strange thing about the voices that I was hearing is, the voices did not sound like the crying of a real baby. These voices in the nights were sometimes shrieking, at other times they were the sounds of a wounded or bleating sheep. In the month of March when we had the abortion, the night voices were so tormenting that I sometimes wished I could exchange my life for hers.

Good and Evil

There are two major forces in the world God, the Father of heavenly lights, grace, love, truth and Satan himself. Both forces are on opposing sides of the abortion issue. While the ancient enemy of God is the lord of abortion; Our Heavenly Father is the Lord God of all life who brings transformation, restoration and elevation from the mangling clutches of His arch enemy in our lives. God is totally and completely opposed to us taking the life of our unborn babies as well as the lives of other human beings. But He is so deeply in-love with us that He spared no expense to condescend to us and redeem us from ALL our painful choices. My aborting brought me to a place of mesmerizing despair and deeper brokenness than I had ever known. One night I asked God to forgive me for my divine law breaking of His sacred statues by taking the life of my baby. I ask the Lord to forgive me for not taking a stronger stand to give her the gift of life. I later forgave myself for these actions. I poured out my all my feelings of shame, guilt, and regrets concerning my own actions in the abortion. I asked my Heavenly Father to forgive me for despising the wonderful blessing of our baby's presence and rejecting His love throughout the whole of my life. I asked Him to forgive me for not embracing the family relationships He gave to us and her life-giving purpose in the earth.

My Father is Dying

When we moved to Florida in July of 1987, I made no attempts to speak with my father. One of my discoveries was wherever I go I take my past with me. I did call Elsa and gave her my contact information. Even though I did not ask about him, she told me that he moved back to Jamaica without her and that she was left alone. Elsa had several health issues, one of which was a heart condition. She wanted to remain in the States for better medical care. The health care needs of his wife did not affect his decision to move back to Jamaica. He moved without any thought or care for her needs. This was another example of my father's total dedication to himself. Late October of 1988 I received a call from Elsa stating that my father was very sick. Elsa told me she was going to Jamaica and bring him back to the States for medical treatment I pondered it in my heart. For while he worked hard and provided, theirs was not a happy union in my view. Elsa was introduced to my father while she was on vacation in Jamaica. A romance followed and after some time, he proposed and gave her a ring and she later came to Jamaica and they were married.

Betrayal

After they were married, she returned to the States and filed for him to get a permanent visa to come and live in the United States. What Elsa did not know is that he had fathered two additional children with another woman in Jamaica while they were courting. He left without the woman knowing he had gotten married and living in the United States. He wrote telling her that he married a woman he did not love to get his legal status in the United States. He further stated after two years he would get a divorce, come to Jamaica, marry her and bring them all to America. In the meantime, he would send financial support for her and the children. Well, in his haste to get to work that morning, he used insufficient postage and the letter returned. Elsa found the letter addressed to another woman in my father's handwriting in their mailbox. So being like any normal woman she opened and read the letter. When she read the contents, she realized she had been had and their love was on the rocks. They stayed together, but she was never able to say more than two civil sentences to him. There was a certain rancor that laced their interactions with each other throughout their marriage. She had been single for many years and was looking forward to a love match, but instead she was used and discarded by my father. My father's betrayal had to be a serious heartbreak for her!

My father was stuck because any attempt to divorce her, the letter to the paramour was proof he married her for a visa. He could have been deported if she pushed the issue with the department of immigration. That was one of the deep senses of betrayal between them. She called to say that he was hospitalized as soon as he came back to America. The doctors found his heart was failing and he had cancer of the pancreas. I later learned that he had Cirrhosis of the Liver and he was given less than six months to live. By now I was a born-again believer and I did not want him to die and go the hell. Well, a small part of me still did for a New York second. After your heart has been changed by God, you want to extend the same forgiveness to everyone even those who still want to be your enemy. I spoke with our pastor and told him that my father was dying of Cirrhosis of the Liver, and he was not a born again. He was very compassionate and told me that they would help me to pray him into the kingdom of God. I told him just enough to let him know there were deep unresolved issues between us. He suggested that I try to make a trip back to New York as soon as I could to see if any reconciliation was possible. I told him I would do that. I really did not want to go knowing how deeply embittered and wounding my father could be, but I kept my promise to the pastor.

My father lived life as lawlessly as he could. He would arise early each morning, read from the Psalms in the Bible as he poured himself drink after drink of Jamaican White Rum, Jamaican Dark Rum, or a variety of whiskeys he kept on hand. He believed he was "god" unto himself. There were many years of grace that he took for granted would always be there and it still was, but would he finally accept it. During the Christmas holiday that year, I travelled to New York with the boys. He was still very angry and did not treat Elsa very well. My two sons stayed at my mother's while I went alone to visit him in hopes that we could make some type of truce before the boys saw their grandpa for the last time. He was still embittered and told me he did not care to see or talk with me even though I had made the trip from Florida to New York to see him on his death bed. I was crushed all over again but grateful to be alone. Both my boys knew who he was, but I still did not wish them to experience any more traumas from him. I left their house in Queens wishing I had not wasted my time to try with him again. I left there thinking this man is beyond pathetic, a poor excuse for a father and a human being!

Obligated to Try

I do not believe that my behaviors towards my father was out of love. It had been drilled into me to honor the position he held of being my biological father. As a girl I had issues with adults demanding honor and respect when they only gave dishonor no matter how much they were honored. It would not have been culturally acceptable, because we are taught to honor our parents no matter what they do against us. And if we ever say to them that their behaviors against us are wrong, verses from the Bible regarding honoring our parents will be quoted and you will be guilty of the greatest wrong against them. My father's bitterness towards me on his death bed felt like I was in the middle of a bitter divorce with the man who biologically fathered me.

While I was visiting for the holidays, I contacted my sister-in-law Princess who lived with me briefly. She invited us to come over, so we drove to Far Rockaway to see their father's side of the family. Princess contacted their father who came to visit his sons at her home. My brother-in-law came to see his nephews and invited us out to China Town for dinner the following evening. We ate the best meal ever in a Chinese Restaurant. He ordered for us and we sampled Chinese cuisine in a way that the boys and I never experienced before, dishes with names I cannot pronounce. We ate to our hearts content and drove back to Florida the following day feeling better for having someone take us out and treat us well.

Impasse with My Father

Upon my return to Florida I spoke with our pastor and told him how the visit went with him. I did not like the situation, but he had chosen to keep it that way. My pastor told me I should not feel responsible for my father's behaviors, only mine. He said, it was my father's responsibility to make the attempts to reconcile with me as his child, but that God saw my efforts and would reward me for trying. About mid-April of 1989 my father called, and we spoke. He said he was sorry for how he acted towards me and I accepted his apology. I prayed with him on the phone and we said our good-byes and God gave me the closure of peace with him that I needed. One week later on April 24, 1989 Elsa called to say my father died. I traveled to New York to his funeral with Graham. Douglas did not attend his funeral and I am grateful that I honored his feelings. The pastor who preached my father's funeral said his last visit with him before he died, he confessed Jesus as his Savior. I felt that at least he would not spend eternity in hell, that our collective prayers were answered for him because we serve a God of infinite grace, mercy, and forgiveness. God relentlessly chased my child molesting, womanizing, and predatory, father to deaths door in order to forgive him. When I saw him laid out in the casket I felt this "cruel, mean, evil, wicked man" who terrorized and tormented me all my life is finally dead, but the journey to healing the traumas that he inflicted throughout my life would begin later.

My Father Died Penniless

One of the things that I learned following my father's funeral is that at the time of his death; he was penniless. So, all of his efforts to manipulate, strive, cheat, scheme, use and discard women was of no benefit to him. Since he died owning nothing, there was no inheritance that his children could rightly claim. When he left her and moved to Jamaica he was chasing "a married bit on the side." Elsa said that all of his fingernails were as black as tar when she went to Jamaica to bring him back to the states for medical care. She believes he was poisoned by the husband of his latest "mistress." My mother who still lived in New York accompanied me to his funeral. The two children that he left in Jamaica were also at his funeral. Elsa was a deeply broken woman by the time he died. So were and me my mother, my sister, my father's only son by the woman he left to marry Elsa to give them a better life. My father Leonard Constantine Hines left many wounded people in the wake of his death. People who would have loved him if only he took the time to notice that what he was searching for was already in his life. Unfortunately, he was never able to see those who had the love he needed because of his lusts for things blinded him and chased him into the grave without possessions in the end. Sad, very sad indeed!

Returned from My Father's Funeral

After I returned from his funeral, I had a major emotional meltdown that was triggered by his death and the wounds from him that I carried. Death is as final as it gets and while he said he was sorry, and I accepted his apology I was in serious pain. A few days after I came back from the funeral, I began to feel seriously suicidal again. My suicidal thoughts became very strong because his death greatly increased my pain level. I called Pastor Will at our church and made an appointment to speak with him. When I met with him, he asked me how things went at the funeral and I told him. I also confided in him that there was an incestuous relationship between me, and my father and his death triggered something I could not handle. He apologized to me for having such a difficult relationship with my father. He said that he had no experience with counseling issues of incest. He prayed with me and ask the Lord to find me someone who would help me find healing. I appreciated that he did not pretend that he had the expertise he did not have on a crucial matter in my life, it showed great integrity on his part.

Loving God

One Sunday evening while I was in our evening service, Pastor Davidson said to the congregation, tell the Lord that you love Him. To my shock and horror, I was unable to utter those words to God. It is not that I was incapable of saying the words; it is that the words held no meaning for me in relationship to God. I thought I have been going to church on and off for so much of my life and not be able to tell God I love Him. The issue of my loving God was not a thought that I recalled hearing although I went to church depending on where I lived. Could it be that all the traumas and pain of my life left me blinded to God's love for me? Yet I did not know that God was supposed to love me or that I was supposed to love Him because the adults in my life did not love me and I knew they did not love me.

Not being taught that God loved me left me without the capacity to receive the love that God wanted to lavish on me. I began to weep as my heart was a-wash with a deep sense of sorrow, grief, pain, and loss. I suddenly realized that I never considered the issue of me loving God or God loving me. I grew up hearing about a God who was exacting, mean-spirited, rejecting, abandoning and punishing with an impervious demand for behaviors without benefits. I got on my hands and knees on the floor of that church and I wept and asked God to forgive me for my indifference towards Him, and for hating myself His creation and He did. I felt hated by my parents because of their abandoning behaviors towards me. Except for Aunt Inez, the people I lived with were very hatefully and indifferent towards me and I towards them sometimes. After I received God's forgiveness, I was finally, for the first time in my life, able to say to God, "I love you" and mean it from my heart.

CHAPTER FOURTEEN

MY VISITATION FROM HEAVEN

I began to have relief from hearing the voices in the nights after I poured my heart out to my Heavenly Father with confession and repentance. This was a welcome relief for me and the pain of not seeing my baby every day began to decrease. By this time, I am seeing a therapist to help me get a perspective on the chaotic and destructive cycles of my life and its devastating impact on my sons. I would cry myself to sleep at night with a broken heart over the pain my sons were suffering, and I was clueless as to how to help them. I often felt that they were living with my pain right along with me the way that I lived with my parent's pain which was the last thing that I wanted for them.

My Vision from Heaven

I was lying in my bed one night when suddenly my bedroom became filled with an incredibly bright and intense light. Within the brilliance of the light there was a figure of a man who was much more than a man. His hair was resplendent white, and His tanned figure was clothed in pristine light which filled my apartment and spilled out into the planet. He was tanned, but He was not a black man; neither was He a tanned white man. A man more than a mere mortal man. Earth has no color of white that is pristine enough to compare to the beauty of His light. He was light in and of Himself. The brilliance of light came from within Him. The Word of God says Jesus is the light of men, but at that

179

point I was not aware of that. He was, is, and will always be the purest of light among men. (John 1:4) In Him was life, and the life was the light of men.

He was covered from his neck to the top of His feet and I saw His scars in His side through His brilliance. His brilliance was not the scars nor the stripes on his back; His brilliance is the healing virtue that transforms the hearts of mankind. It is the essence of His cross. While His scares could be identified, they were not His persona or identity. What He allowed to be broken has been completely renewed and He walked in the newness of His resurrected Body as we do by faith when we accept His finished work on the Cross. The true essence of His love is death on the Cross and His not the brokenness that He left behind, but the power of His resurrected life. His feet did not touch the floor of my bedroom. He stood over me by the foot of my bed, suspended in midair. Yet He was solid, stable, and balanced at the same time. My thoughts wondered for a moment as to why and how could a figure of a man stand supported and suspended above ground all by himself. The brilliance of His light quickly drew me back to His presence and away from my human thoughts.

Essence of Love

As I looked at His face, He was smiling deeply. He was peaceful and the love that I felt coming from Him was a pure undefiled love that liberated me of my wrong doings. I wanted to touch His light, touch His love, touch His face but as His presence engulfed me, I was speechless and motionless that He cared for me so deeply. The love coming from Him enveloped and enfolded me so profoundly I wanted to stay there forever. In the presence of His love and light I felt free and without fear. I knew in an instant He was not there to hurt or harm me. He came to restore the broken pieces of my life. He was human and He was divine; fully man and fully God. I have known intimate moments in His presence since then, but not like that night when He appeared to me in my vision.

How purely intimate! This love coming from my King was so much deeper than what I saw that morning when I accepted

Christ at First Assembly of God in Ocala, Florida. As I looked into crook of His left arm, I saw an infant wrapped in the same pristine white without beginning or end. He looked into my eyes and said; "She is here with us there is no need to sorrow for her, be at peace, for she is safe and alive." I felt water drizzling down my cheek as He spoke tenderly about my daughter whose life we had taken. Then my focus shifted to the prettiest, cutest, most beautiful brown baby that I have ever seen. She was first an infant in His arms, but as I looked and tried to take in all that I was experiencing, she suddenly began to grow from an infant, to a toddler crawling, then taking her first step, and then becoming a beautiful adolescent girl. My tears continued to drizzle in stillness of motion in the presence of my King, JESUS. All that was within me stood still in the presence of the Lord and my daughter. Jesus restored the years I had missed in the stages of Mercella's life. Who but a loving Heavenly Father could make all things I attempted to destroy new and beautiful in His time?

This experience was in March of 1988. Our daughter was aborted on March the 17th of 1975. Mercella was thirteen years old at the time Jesus appeared to me in my vision. She had the Father, the Son, the Holy Spirit, along with millions of Moms and Dads to love her in heaven. I continued to drizzle, but my drizzling was free from pain, sorrow, sadness, hurt, guilt, or shame. I felt completely embraced and accepted in the brilliance of His enfolding essence. It brought me to a place of peace that is beyond my ability to express.

My Apostasy

Following my vision, I became aware that the number thirteen was significant. Why would Jesus come to me in the thirteenth year after we had the abortion? It had to mean something, but what? I looked up the meaning of the number thirteen and found many definitions; however, they did not represent the meaning of the message Jesus gave in my vision. I spent some time pondering and praying about the significance of the number thirteen. Then I recalled reading a book earlier in the year entitled "The SEER", written by Jim W. Goll, who is a prophetic intercessor.

181

I purchased the book some years ago and read it. However, in January 2014 I felt a nudge to read it again. The significance of the number thirteen from a Biblical perspective represents: rebellion, backsliding, and apostasy of God's people against our Creator. The principle of "first mention" sets the standard for Biblical interpretation throughout the Bible. In my vision Jesus was speaking to my state of apostasy which was our renunciation of religious faith and us embracing the choice of abortion over the provisions of God's gift of love.

The personal significance of the thirteenth year in my vision is that God intervened in my life and kept His hand on me constantly. When it was demanded that I do the unthinkable with my first born I stood my ground, holding firm to my own personal beliefs. He protected me, made ways for me, watched over me the night I went into labor and delivered both of us alive. My Heavenly Father did so much for me, and I continued to be so blinded by the neglect of my past to the love of God. I kept looking to myself to make my own way in the world rather than seek the way God had for me. I did not see Him the same way Lot could not see his need for God, so he looked to himself. This deception began in the Garden of Eden when Eve who had the perfect life was beguiled by the intellectual prowess of the ancient enemy of God and accepted his lies that God was not good to her, so she needed to find her own way in life. He basically convinced her that she could do better for herself than our Creator had already done for her and all of humanity. By the time I was faced with the same scenario the second time I had renounced God. To be more precise my spirit had dumped God and the fear of Him was not a factor for me by this time as it was with my first-born son's conception.

With Douglas I based my decision on my own self will to keep my baby, in the case of Mercella my will was too splintered to maintain any of its own integrity against these attacks. This issue of my spirit and soul being fractured would not be addressed until I was hospitalized from a total emotional and spiritual meltdown. It was then that I was able to come full circle with myself and I saw for the first time how much my Creator had invested in me from my very "humble beginnings." It was there that I began to see my life as having meaning, design, destiny, and purpose. I was there in the place of my complete collapse that I was able to see the protection, mercy, undeserved grace, and goodness of God in all of my issues. It was there that I saw how much of His mercy and protection that I had taken for granted.

Heaven's Redemption

Just before my Lord turned to leave, the vision began to expand, and I saw all around Jesus a numberless host of children of all ages, sizes, races, cultures, and ethnicities. Then He said, they are all here with us; all of the aborted children are here with us, safe and alive in our care. I immediately understood that it was not only our daughter whom He watched over to protect, but countless mothers and fathers who embraced "choice." He, our Creator stepped in and transformed, restored, and elevated our tragic choices into beautiful pure white pearls of blessings in heaven. I began to weep as His presence left me just as gently and as quietly as He appeared. He was gone, but the message that His visit came to impart was clear and it made such an impact on me that I have never forgotten it. I do not know how long this experience lasted, it seemed like only a moment in time, but it changed my life forever. Even as I am writing this account today, I am reminded of a chorus that I learned at First Assembly of God in Ocala, Florida: "Lord I stand, I stand in awe of you. Lord I stand; I stand in awe of you. Holy God to whom ALL praise is due. I stand in awe of you, I stand in awe of you, and I stand in awe of you.

I could not physically stand, but my heart stood to attention at the awesome wonder of my Lord and King, Jesus-the-Christ. Thinking back on the experience, I still cannot articulate how it felt to be there in the presence of the pure love of God. His presence spoke in volumes too immense to be overlooked. In the same manner that women and men everywhere know in our hearts and souls they are aborting a baby. If we never heard a sermon on abortion, we have an inner sense we are crossing a boundary that is divine in scope and magnitude. Each of us do the unthinkable for our own reasons and rationalizations. This is one of the questions of self-evaluation that each of us must answer before the healing of our self-inflicted traumas of our abortion will be complete.

I did not have any questions and I still do not understand why He chose to appear to me in such a manner. I am grateful that He did. It gave me the ability to breathe a breath of healing that I had not known since that day in March of 1975. When I was awakened, my senses were stirred. I felt more alive than before and I had peace that I was completely forgiven and free from any condemnation in aborting our baby. Somehow this encounter suddenly closed the rawness of the open, oozing, cankerous wounds that filled my being with its defilement and torment for years following the moment in time of our abortion. I had hoped and prayed that she was in heaven with Jesus and He assured me in my vision from heaven that she was with Him. How awesome is our God!

My Daughter is Beautiful

When I looked at my daughter as she grew, I could see my beauty in her. Her movements resembled mine at different stages of my life. I gave my daughter the name Mercella in honor of my Aunt Inez who showed mercy and grace to me and any hurting child that crossed her path. I chose March 17th, 1975 as redeeming the date in celebration of her life and her birth. Each year I rejoice and honor her life in quiet stillness of the gentle spirit that my Heavenly Father has restored to us. There is a longing that only the blessing of her presence will satisfy when I see her in heaven someday. I am so grateful that my daughter and I will be spending eternity together in-spite-of my choice to abort her. Following my vision from heaven, my therapist felt it would lead me to deeper closure to write a letter to my daughter and it did.

My Letter to my Daughter, Mercella, in Heaven

My Sweet Brown Baby Girl,

I write this letter to you today in front of all heaven, earth, and hell calling attention to the fact that I am telling God the Father, God the Son, and Holy Spirit that I am sorry for aborting your life and destiny on the earth. Jesus has already forgiven me and now I am asking you to forgive me for taking your life, it was not ours to take. You were created in the express image of God and you were a gift to our family, to yourself and to the world. You were given to us as a sacred trust by our Father in heaven and we failed to carry out our keeping responsibility. I do not know who you were to be, but I believe that you would have been a blessing on the earth through whom your Heavenly Father would live His life. I am also forgiving myself for choosing to keep your father in my life rather than honoring your life and presence. I believe that you were designed to do something very special in the earth that will never be done because your life was taken. While you have always been in Our Father's care, today I willingly release you to Him. Your brothers' would have loved you their little sister very much. I will look for you as soon as I embrace Jesus in heaven. We will sit and talk about whatever people talk about in heaven. I will need you to teach me about heaven and take me on a tour of your special sights growing up in heaven. Our Heavenly Father made you a beautiful pearl of pure blessing in His Kingdom. Goodbye for now, I will be with you in heaven someday.

Your Mom

I did not share this vision with anyone except for my therapist for many years. There was the sense that this vision from heaven of my daughter Mercella being restored to me was my personal treasure. I did not want the sacredness of the vision to be contaminated by the opinions of people. Jesus brought her back to me. She became real to me and I needed to keep my baby close in my heart alone. She was a thirteen-year-old beautify enrobed and safe in heaven.

Post Abortion Stressors

I encourage each woman who has had an abortion and men who know that they are part of the decision to abort, to sit down and make a list of all the issues of your life that became stagnant and stubbornly unmanageable after you have had the abortion. Issues that were not a part of your family's heritage that have now become a stumbling block in all aspects of your life. Look at issues such as increased drinking, drug use, increases in destructive behaviors such as suicide, abuses that you allow to take place that you would not have allowed before the abortion. Have you experienced several miscarriages since the abortion? Have you developed a cold hardened edge against men and women since the abortion? Are you very bitter with men since the abortion? Are you bitter with women and with yourself since a woman aborted your baby? Do you feel emotionally and spiritually numb or de-sensitized since having an abortion? All of these are behaviors that represent an array of issues that women and men find themselves experiencing as post abortion stressors.

The above are some of the core issues that I have found in my life. As a therapist I have observed men, women of all cultures, ethnicities and socio-economic status experiencing some of these issues. As I have been able to process my grief, I find I am more open to discussing the issue of abortion without feeling shame. Many women have shared with me about having an abortion while married. They did it to keep their marriages only to lose the marriage over the process of time. This comes down to rejection and abandonment by a man who they are in a relationship with. Married Christian and non-Christian women are having abortions is not an anomaly, it is a daily occurrence across the world and in all walks of life.

Forgiving My Ex-husband

One evening while working on this book, I received a call from my friend and fellow intercessor that lives in Florida. I began to share with her how I was doing. She is an awesome woman of God who operates in the Word of knowledge from the Lord; and one that the Lord has put in my life and me in her life for such a time as this. We have walked with each other through some of life's challenges in prayer and with encouraging words. I shared with her about the writing of this book, and as we talked the Holy Spirit revealed that I still had not yet forgiven my ex-husband for demanding that we have an abortion. I began to weep as I felt floods of memories concerning his behaviors against my opinion to abort our baby washed over me, so we prayed the following prayer.

Heavenly Father, I do not forgive my ex-husband because I feel like it, but I forgive him out of obedience to your word. However, this time my forgiveness will be from the heart which is a process that takes time. It depends on the levels of wounding that we have experienced and the length of time the hurts have been buried alive in our subconscious minds for heart forgiveness to be accomplished. So, by an act of my will I choose to obey Your Word and forgive him. I also forgive myself for not being true to my own feelings because of my fears of being abandoned and rejected again.

CHAPTER FIFTEEN

JOURNEY TO WHOLENESS AND TRANSFORMATION

During the years that I lived in Florida and was attending church, I experienced a long period of time when I did not have any suicidal thoughts or feelings. For some reason as Graham was in his senior year in high school, I began to feel myself coming unglued or unhinged. It became more and more difficult for me to maintain the stability that I had gained. I knew that it was not post-abortive issues because the vision from heaven had settled all of that. It is against this backdrop that I tried to drive my car into a ditch at a construction site one day when Graham was in high school. When my car came to the edge of the ditch, it suddenly stopped and would not move. No matter how much I floored my gas pedal the tires only kept spinning, but the vehicle would not move forward.

I put my head on my steering wheel with my car in drive and began to scream. I asked God to let me die because my life was a complete failure. I said, God if you cannot heal my pain please just let me die. I attempted to drive my car forward again, but it would not move. So, I put the car in reverse, and it jump back from the edge. I drove home still feeling very hopeless, but glad it did not work because Graham would be in a city by himself abandoned by the suicide of his mother. As the nightmares, flashbacks, and memories of my childhood continued to invade my consciousness, I began to long for death more and more. I was afraid to share with my church family that I was again having suicidal thoughts. I also continued to struggle to maintain my employment because of missed days from work. I could not explain the thoughts I was having so I could resign one position and get unemployment for a few months. I was hoping that the rest would help but it did not.

After overhearing an argument between me and his father on the telephone about child support, Graham said Mom, you'll see, Dad will come through when he sees that I am a good kid. I am an honor student, I am graduating from high school, I have not gotten into trouble, and I am headed to college. I going to Boy's State. Boys State is a leadership program in Florida where boys who are qualified attend and participate in a mock legislative process of the state for one week. They develop a working knowledge of the structure of government to impress upon them that the government is what we the citizenry make of it. He is going to come through for me Mom you will see. He was basing this on his father attending Douglas's graduation in New York after ignoring them both. I do not know if Graham contacted his father and let him know that he was graduating.

I understood Graham's need for the validation of his father the same way that I needed my father's and mother's validation upon my graduation from college. When I graduated and my father and mother stood proud that day on the Green at the Rose Hill Campus of Fordham University, it was a priceless feeling that healed some things in me. It is no doubt the reason it was not hard for my father to convince me to move to Queens. However, while I saw his behaviors as an act of maturity and change, he had other motives. It still felt good to have him and my mother together for one of my big days. I made several attempts to contact his father in New York, but he never responded concerning the issue of Graham's graduation from high school. I finally spoke with his wife a few days before graduation and she told me that he had received the messages I left for him. She did not know if he was coming to his son's graduation. I knew that meant he would not be there.

Missing Again

The night before Graham's graduation I made one last attempt to contact his father, but I only got his answering machine. He was missing at his son's graduation and Graham was deeply hurt and so was I. I did all I knew to do to get him to respond in a positive manner. I stood in the stands and cheered very loudly when Graham's name was called. I was both proud of him and impress with him for his academic achievements, involvement in sports, and participation in Boys State. Following the graduation ceremonies Graham chose to go out with his friends rather than going to dinner with me. I went home and cried that night that Graham came this far without his Dad and he still could not do this one thing for his biological son.

About October of 1992 following Graham's graduation; his father finally called to say he did not receive the messages because he was out of the country. "Your wife told me that you received the messages." Oh, she did? She does not know what she is talking about. I do not tell her anything about my business." I told him that Graham graduated with honors just like Douglas and was at college up in Gainesville, Florida. Graham worked a morning job from 4 am to 8 am then drove my car to Gainesville from Ocala to school. The conversation suddenly turned ugly when I asked him to assist me with Graham's college tuition. I don't have any money was the reply. So being good and angry, I weighed in deep. "You don't have any money for your only son's tuition, but I bet you would have no problem finding money for one of your "bits" on the side. I am not working, and our son needs your help to get him through the rest of the way. He has worked very hard, done very well, he is a good boy, and he wanted and needed your approval. Being there would have been endorsement that spoke in volumes to him about your love for him. He is your biological son and you have ignored him most of his life. He was very disappointed and deeply wounded when you did not show up for his graduation. It was a very special day for him, and he not only needed you there, he wanted you there." Well, went downhill and I or both of us hung up. I gave Graham the message that his Dad called and edited all my venting. I never asked Graham if he called his father back and he never said.

He! Takes Me to Court

In May of 1993 one year after Graham's graduation from high school, I received a summons from Child Support Enforcement in the Bronx, New York. He filed a petition in court to dismiss the Child Support Order and cancel the arrears that he owed because Graham was now going to be nineteen years old. Florida's law stops child support after eighteen unless the child is still in high school graduating before age 19, but in the state of New York the law required the non-custodial parent is responsible to pay child support until the child is twenty-one. When I received the summons, I was just ready to forget all about his being a "dead beat Dad." I was emotionally exhausted and becoming disconnected from the injustices of my life. I showed the letter to Graham because he saw the address and knew it was about child support. We had lost our apartment and we were staying with a friend at the time.

For whatever reason Graham was not aware of all the steps I had taken to get his father to be a responsible parent. When you live in a different state and the one who pays child support is working off the books it is quite difficult to collect. When I showed the letter to Graham, he read it, and became angry and said: "Mom, you need to go and fight him on this." I also received a call from the Child Support Enforcement Unit in New York asking me to come to court or it would be laid aside because their efforts were not paying off with him. She explained to me that my ex-husband believes he was not responsible to pay child support so they needed me to come so that the judge could rule that he was responsible.

I thought his father would be proud of his son following in his footsteps. My ex-husband told me a story once about his father being taken to court by his mother for child support for him in Jamaica. On the day of the child support hearing in, he stated that his father refused to go to court so his Mom lost the case. Graham and I discussed the issue and he were upset that his father still did not want to contribute to his care. My furniture was already in storage with a friend and Graham wanted to go and visit with Douglas in California who had recently returned from Desert Storm in Iraq. I would be staying with my sister Rachel and her family in South Jersey. The plan was for me to come to court in New York and follow the process through. Graham on the other hand would get a summer job in California, help his brother out and save as much as possible to help with his school expenses when we returned to Florida that August.

Douglas Gets out of the Navy

Douglas was honorably discharged from the United States Navy after his tour of duty in Iraq and the brothers wanted to spend some time together over the summer. I was concerned about Graham especially since his Dad ignored him for most of his life and was missing for his big day after he worked so hard. Being ignored by any parent is a "type "B" trauma. Graham went to California to see Douglas at the end of May and I went to South Jersey. We kept in touch and Graham wanted to know what happened each time I went to court, and we all spoke weekly. Each time I would call he would say he was not yet working, and this greatly concerned me. I kept praying and encouraging him to find a summer job. On the days that I had court at the Bronx Family Court I spent the nights at my mother to get there early in the morning. These court appearances were an all-day waiting process.

Shocked

At my first appearance at court, he showed up and it was very obviously shocked to see me answering his summons. He wanted to speak with me outside and I listened. "Vivienne why don't you drop the whole matter so that I can get my import/export license in New York. They denied my application because I owe you child support which I am not supposed to pay." I politely said, "Pay me what you owe me, and the matter will be over." I was just supposed to drop the issue so that he could get what he wanted for himself. As I listened to him, I realized that nothing had change about him over the years. He was still the same self-centered predator he always was. I still expected me to "grin and bear" while he continued to deprive my sons of what was rightfully theirs without a final fight. He still had not learned after almost twenty years that he needed to be responsible for his children. When I refused to drop the case, he left in a rage! Go figure! I stayed until the case of was called. When I appeared before the judge, he asked me if my ex-husband was present and I told him that he was here earlier. He sent the bailiff to call his name and when he did not answer the case was rescheduled. Graham called me that night to ask what happened and I told him about the conversation with his Dad and that he did not stay for the case to be called, so it was rescheduled. He wanted to know if I was staying to see it through and I told him that I was.

Endurance Race

I had learned over the years with him that everything was an endurance race. I stayed in New York for five months because the case was rescheduled each time he did not show up. The case was rescheduled four time, but he never showed up. On my fifth court appearance the judge gave me the option to keep coming to court or take a final judgment. The judge explained that his case had no merit because non-custodial parent is responsible until the minor child is 21, but if I was not there it could have been dismissed. The judge also stated that it did not matter where I lived because the case was in New York and the laws of New York required him to pay child support of his son until he turned twenty-one. I took the final judgment because I knew him well enough to know he would never show his face again and "man up." Being a man who was accountable is not who he was! Only a mature man can "man-up" to his child support responsibility and he was not in that category of manhood. Better knowing late than never knowing who you hooked up with and had children with them.

He felt that since I was in Florida, he had the cards stacked against me and he would be legally free from child support. This time he was hoping for an easy kill because I would not show up to court. When I showed up, he knew he had already lost because I would fight to the finish. I took the paperwork for my final judgment and went to the Sheriff's Office on the Grand Concourse and filed the papers immediately after leaving court. When I got home to South Jersey Graham called to learn if his Dad showed up in court and I had to tell him the truth. "No, your Dad did not show up." I told him that I took the offer for a final judgment which the judge made, and I already filed the papers with the Sheriff's Office.

He was not happy, but I told him if your father filed any income tax return, we will be getting those funds. Graham knew that his Dad went for years not filing income tax returns. We talked about returning to Florida and I discussed sending him a plane ticket to Florida. We were going to stay with a friend for a few weeks while we found a place and resumed our lives. He was returning to the University of Florida in Gainesville as a sophomore. I was aware that Douglas was not going to be home that week, but he would check in when he got back about the court issue with his father. I received the call from Douglas on a Wednesday in August 1993. I was expecting Douglas to ask about the court case. Instead he told me that he came home, and Graham had taken his clothes and his comic books and left. I spoke with Graham on Monday the final court date, so he either took off after we talked, or he left on that Tuesday. Douglas was very upset that there was no note and no sign of foul play.

Graham Went Missing August 1993

For Graham, taking his comic books was very serious. He had a collection of comic books that was worth some money. They were his most prized possessions which he had been collecting for years. Graham was simply gone, and no one knew where. Douglas did some inquiring but could not get any concrete information. Graham is a deeply introspective intelligent young person who had many friends, but always seemed to be able to outthink others in a good way. Graham could also hold his own in any conversation with adults because he was well read and smart like his big brother Douglas. However, smart individuals sometimes make foolish choices when they are hurting, and my sons was in a world of hurt that had been stirred up that summer. I went to Bible Study that night at Fountain of Life Church in Burlington, New Jersey. During praise and worship service I went to the altar and I began to pour my heart out before the Lord. I heard the Holy Spirit say, "he has not left you; he is running from me like Jonah." During Graham's freshman year in college he asked me one Sunday morning on our way to church, "Mom, what would you do if God called you to do something, but you had other plans for your life?" I said to my son. "Say yes to the calling of God on your life and He will give you your desires also. I asked him if he knew what God called him to do. "Yes" was Graham's response! My next question was: what is it that God is calling you to do? Graham became quiet and would not answer. I remember praying in my heart as we continued to drive that the Holy Spirit would soften his heart to follow the path that His Heavenly Father had chosen for him.

California to Find My Son

Shortly after the phone call from Douglas I went to California to see if I could find Graham and to become reunited with Douglas who was recently out of the Navy. I went to the police station to file a missing person report, but I learned I could not do that. The police said; "your son is eighteen years old and he has the right to go anywhere he chooses. We can't allow you to file a missing person's report unless you suspect foul play" and we did not. Douglas and I went to some places he might be, but we came up empty. While I was there Douglas and I reconnected as we attempted to learn about Graham's whereabouts. I returned to Florida in October still not knowing and feeling as if I had failed my children miserably. I continued to pray and hire private detectives, but I came up empty every time. I was already on temporary disability because I was not able to return to work and my finances were running low. The issues of my childhood and my adult life finally became so emotionally debilitating that I was unable to work for a few years.

My Return to Florida

After I returned to Florida, I got an apartment and continued to attend church at First Assembly of God and returned to therapy two hours each week. It was during this time that I became extremely depressed and lethally suicidal. Over the years I would have occasional flashbacks but now they were daily intrusive episodes. I would wake up at night screaming in a cold sweat of memories that were constant and frightening. Praying, reading scriptures, and binding did very little to stem the tide of these engulfing assault of past ghost on my emotions. I felt as if I was still in the warzone with my past and I was losing the war this time around. I could not go for more than one hour without an intrusive assault of memories from my past overwhelming me. I had been free from thoughts and feelings of suicide for a long-time then suddenly there they were again in living color and continuous motion.

I planned my suicide again to make sure it would work, so I bought a package of razor blades to complete my plan. I made sure to clean so that my dead body would not be found in a dirty apartment, my laundry was done and folded neatly and put away. My boys were not at home at the time. Graham was missing and Douglas was in California struggling to find his way after coming home from the war in Iraq. I began to compare myself with my parents and I was coming out looking worse than they because my thinking became corrupted. In addition, the ancient enemy who wanted me dead throughout the whole of my life was capitalizing on my circumstances to get me to take myself out once and for all. Satan could not kill me because he never had the legal right. However, if he could combine the totality of my life's pain and failures, he might get me to push my own death button through my crippling panic and fear. Being buried alive placed a spirit of death inside my psychological network so that the ancient enemy of God could keep taking me back to a place of death as the best solution when it was NOT. The ancient enemy of God can only do in my life what I determine of my "free will" to do IF I listened to his lies.

My Hospitalization

When I missed my appointment with my therapist that week, she became worried and contacted me because she knew I was not doing well and was very concerned. During our conversation she gave me an ultimatum. She had been trying to get me into a specialized unit for incest survivors with satanic ritual abuse for some time, but I kept refusing to go. I was stuck on the point where she said I had experienced ritual abuses as a child growing up. I was buried alive but at the time I did not accept that it was part of ritual satanic abuses even though it was. My therapist said if I did not go to the specialized hospital unit where they could help me work through my past in a safe environment, she would have me committed to an inpatient psychiatric unit. She also asked me to flush the razor blades down the toilet, which I did. My therapist said that the enemy was using the issues of my past and what was going on with my children to take me out and release death on my sons. She believed that God allowed my complete meltdown so that He could totally heal my past and take me into a brighter future. A future where the past was nailed to the foot of the cross and unable to come back to haunt and torment me at will because I was healed and free from its mind blinding shackles.

Being committed by my therapist would have taken away some of my options of freedom which I value highly. So, I volunteered, and she made the arrangements. Just to make sure I would go she called the police and asked them to come and check on me periodically. They called me each week until I was safely in the hospital. My therapist felt that I needed to trust someone in my faith community to help pray me through while I was in the hospital. After very careful consideration I asked the wife of our pastor and she agreed to pray for me as I walked through my healing process. Lady Davidson prayed for me and I never heard any of my business in the congregation. I also called Douglas in California and told him I was being hospitalized because of the issues of my past. I did not want to burden him with the details of being currently suicidal.

While I was in this specialized unit, I learned a great deal about myself and the struggles I went through the whole of my life. Most importantly I learned that I could really heal from my past. This staff was very knowledgeable about satanic ritual abuses and its aftermath in my life and they gave me hope. I also learned that my healing was a journey rather than a destination. I learned that God is not interested in me forgetting my past, He wants to heal my past by bringing wholeness: transforming my human spirit, soul and body. After I was home from the hospital, Douglas called and wanted to come home and I said yes. He got a job in Ocala, Florida driving a truck which paid him well. He also completed his education after dropping out of Morehouse College. If God takes away our past in the healing process, we would lose our wisdom that comes from our struggles and be unable to identify with others.

Lessons Learned

While I was at the hospital, I was diagnosed with severe Post Traumatic Stress Disorder/PTSD and Bipolar Disorder 1. I learned that the adults in my world growing up had major issues which traumatized my human spirit and will to the extreme and left me with very few healthy coping skills. I was very good at survival but the skills we employ during combat are only good for the battlefield. Once the battle was over, I needed new life skills which I was not trained to develop during my survival days. There was also no room for me to develop new life skills because the abuses continued into my adulthood which kept me stuck going from one traumatic event after the other with the lies that were embedded in each traumatic event in my traumatized brain. I went from one chaotic crisis to another always surviving bur never being able to catch my breath between crises and begin to thrive. I accepted that I was not an inherently bad person and that I was responsible for my behaviors NOT the toxic behaviors of my parents, the adults who refused to love and care for me, or for my ex-husband's abuses and neglect of me and our sons. My hospital experience gave me hope and taught me I still had a mountain of recovery to climb and that I would be a success in my life because somehow God had a purpose for me. I learned that I was not crazy or losing my grip on reality I was a traumatized woman from the experiences of my past.

After My Hospitalization

A group of us founded a stock club where we all pooled and invested $50 each month and purchased stocks. The club members began wanting a change, so we sold all our stock portfolio and divided the proceeds equally among us. By that time, I had returned to work full-time in Daytona Beach, Florida while I still lived in Ocala, Florida. That was a long commute every day to and from work. I used my share of the funds from the stock club to put a down payment on a condo in Daytona Beach, Florida and moved there to be closer to work. I returned to school and got a degree in Advanced Addictions Studies at the NET Institute in Titusville, Florida. It was necessary for me to pass two certification exams to become a Certified Addictions Professional in Florida which I did.

I returned to school again and received a Master's of Science in Marriage and Family Therapy from Stetson University in Deland, Florida graduating in 2004. While at Stetson I became a member of Chi Sigma Iota a Counseling & Academic Professional Honor Society International by invitation. I worked my way up from an internship to a supervisory position then started my own business providing addictions services to families in the Daytona Beach area working under licensed supervision. I became active in my secular community as well as my church community. When I returned to work after my hospitalization and recovery I was chosen as employee of the Year in November 2002 from Serenity House of Volusia County. Then I also receive an award for outstanding support to the Volusia County Dependency Drug Court Program in 2004 in Daytona Beach, Florida.

Esther's Cottage a Radio Ministry

I started a radio ministry with my pastor's blessings on Saturday mornings to share my testimony and Douglas would sometimes join me on the program. I began to feel an urging in me to move, but moving back to New York, it was a painful decision and process, but I was able to do the land cleansing that was necessary for break through hearing from Graham. While I was in the process of seeking the Lord about where he was moving me, I had to have emergency surgery for a tumor which turned out to be pre-cancerous. In addition, my doctor found so much scar tissue inside of me that had to be cleaned out that he said to me after surgery, I have never seen so much scar tissues in any woman in over twenty years of being a surgeon. My physical recovery was now very extended, and I was self-employed. I had poured most of my financial resources into the business. I had no income because I could not work. To keep from losing my investment I sold my condo in Daytona Beach, Florida. I used some of the proceeds from the sale to pay off my medical and business expenses before moving to New York.

EPILOGUE

I received a few telephone calls from the officers of the Los Angeles Police Department requesting blood for DNA comparison periodically. They wanted to use a sample for comparison with young black men in the morgue to determine if Graham was there. I absolutely refused! When he was unable to persuade me, the officer asked me, "are you one of those mothers who pray?" Yes sir. "Only a mother like you would believe that after over sixteen years of not seeing or hearing from your son that he is still alive." I said to the officer, I do understand what you are saying and how you feel. You think that I am certifiable and that I need a mental health evaluation for believing my son is alive.

He did not respond, but I could hear him nodding in my spirit with a smirk. "I went on to say to him, I work in the field of mental health and if I were you speaking to me, I would have those same feelings. BUT my son is alive, and I know it! I cannot prove it yet, but I know that he is alive and, on the planet, somewhere and I will not have you look in the morgue to see if he is there. I know that he is NOT there, and my spirit knows it!" When I hung up the phone I quoted. Now Faith is the substance of things hoped for the evidence of things not seen. (Hebrew 11:1) After that they never again contacted me to ask for a DNA sample so that they could check the morgue for my son. On June 16, 2012 I was pacing back and forth long after my morning devotion, feeling a deep anguish over Graham being missing for almost nineteen years. While it appeared, Graham fell off the planet, I believed in my spirit that he was alive, and until my spirit or God said differently, Graham was alive! Continuing to believe was sometimes difficult and I would cry out to God saying, "I do not understand but by an act of my will I choose to trust you that my son is alive and that he will be home!"

I received a call from the Los Angeles Police Department on June 23, 2012 one week later that my son was being taken off the missing person's list because he was very much alive, well and would be released later that day on his own. He was arrested on a misdemeanor charge for getting in the officer's way while the officer attempting to perform his duty. Do not ask me what duties I do not know, and I do not care, MY SON GRAHAM IS ALIVE! MY SON GRAHAM IS ALIVE! Glory, Glory, Glory, Glory, Glory, Glory, Glory to GOD!!!

I was given the information to contact the jail directly for further information about him. When I called, I was told that he could not receive any information from the officers. I wanted him to get my telephone number in New York, where I was living at the time. After I moved to New York I refused to change my telephone number until I heard that Graham was alive. That was the only contact that the Los Angeles Police Department had for reaching me. I pleaded with the officer and told her that I have not seen nor heard from my boy in nineteen years. If there was any assistance that she could provide for me I would be very grateful. I called my son in Florida back and he suggested that I contact the jail's Chaplin. When you are in crisis your emotions are out of range and this is a very normal response, so I made no effort to be professional. I am a Mom who just learned my "son is very much alive after almost nineteen years of silence.

I was in such intense emotional turmoil that I was unable to think clearly and had to be directed by Douglas. When I contacted the jail Chaplin's office, he was off that day. I called the officer back and asked if she would take my information and pass it on to the Chaplin when he returned to work the following day and she did. When I called back later to learn if he was released, I learned he was not only released they had given Graham my telephone number. To God be all the GLORY. I don't know how God got that to happen, but I pray a special blessing on all those who were involved in getting my information to my son Graham.

I called my sisters and my brother to tell them the excellent news. "My Graham is Alive!" I called his grandmother in Jamaica who was overjoyed as she was praying and believing with me that he was alive. I called First Assembly of God in Ocala, Florida where we all got saved, and they were overjoyed to hear he was alive and placed him back on the Prayer Chain. I called the church that I attended when I moved to Daytona Beach, Florida. I called the church that I attended in South Jersey and I asked everyone to give them my praise report and to pray that he would contact me. Everyone was celebrating this grand and glorious news of Graham being alive with me. Many people were also surprised to hear he was alive after all this time. I kept hearing, you never stopped believing he was still alive.

On June 27th, 2012 about 10:30 in the morning my phone rang and when I answered the person hung up. I knew in my heart that it was Graham. So, I immediately began to pray again that he would call me back and he did in a few minutes later. We talked for several minutes, he apologized for not contacting me and I told him I have already forgiven him. We talked about some of the family members, including his brother, and he mentioned his grandmother and I told him that she was in the States for medical care and would love to see him. He asked me how old his grandmother was. She is eighty-six, I said to him. I asked him if I could come and visit him and he said no. I invited him to come home even if it was only for a visit and he was not ready to do that either. I was very elated to hear from him, but disappointed that he was still not ready to come home. While I disagreed with him about coming home, he is an adult man not the nineteen-year-old college sophomore who went to California to visit his brother for the summer. I cried for the joy of knowing he was alive, and I spoke to him and heard his voice. I also cried because he was not ready to return to the family that was lovingly waiting and praying for him.

Graham not being ready to come home was a heartbreaking moment, but I felt that I should give Graham the space and time that he needed to come home when he is ready. So, I continue to wait for his return to me and a complete restoration of our family.

I have heard of many reasons why missing sons and daughters are afraid to go back home even for a visit. Reasons such as fear of questioning, rejection, guilt, shame, or anger from some family members. I know that the same God who kept him all these years will continue to keep him and restore him to us. I continue to wait and trust in the restorative justice and wisdom of my Heavenly Father to heal and restore my family.

My son Douglas told me that he is grateful that I did not listen to his father and grandfather and abort him. He shared that in-spite of how difficult life was growing up for him, he is very happy to be alive. This statement from my son is worth more than its weight in gold and validates the pain of being abandoned when I chose to maintain my values and give him the opportunity to have a life.

CHAPTER NOTES

Hebrews 11:1

John 1:4-5

Type "C" Trauma

I named trauma: Type "C" Trauma –Type "C" Is when a traumatized individual inflects more trauma on themselves, because TRAUMA that is buried ALIVE stays alive and creates more cycles of traumatic events in OUR lives.

Glossary of some Jamaican Patios and Proverbs

Bit on the side –mistress, concubine, hairy bank, a man in a relationship with woman who is not his wife

Bulla – a round thick sweet ginger cake

Bush tea – herbal tea

Black pan abortion – an illegal abortion in a back room unsafe condition.

Being Cross – is an attitude such as hostility, anger, and aggression against someone.

Dadda, Dad, or Pops, – father

Domino – board game

Dulcemina Grip – a small brown very sturdy suitcase

Grannie or Grammie – grandmother

Grip – suitcase

Hairy bank – reference to men especially married men using their money to womanize wasting their substance outside of their marriage

Hard dough Bread – Jamaican bread. Very delicious when hot with butter. When it's stale, it's hard.

Heavy Mannas – being under intense oppression in one's marriage or any predatory relationship or situation

Higglah – usually a woman who makes her living selling in the Jamaican market

Hand a-akimbo – hand on the hip telling someone off

If you want good your nose has to run – it takes sacrifices to achieve your goals.

June Plum Tree – white or like California cherries

Ludy – a board game that Jamaicans play. The board is self-made and played with a dice.

Mamah – or Mudda, Mumma Mother

Obeah – witchcraft, evil

Partnah/Partner – This is an agreement formed between a few people to put a specific amount into a pool each week. Every week someone from the group gets to 'draw' the total from the pool. The number of people in the pool in most cases determines the number of weeks the pool lasts before a new cycle. Every person must get a draw.

Renk – is foul smell, to be rude

Pit toilet – out house

Tie head – a scarf or bandana used to cover women's head.

Trace – to be told off, cussed out

Vex – angry, upset, and mad

When family finger stink, you can't cut it off and throw it away – sometimes family members have issues, but do not cut them off or throw them away, work with them, if they will allow you, if not love them from a far.

Where ignorance is "bliss", it is folly to be wise – wisdom is not available to those who choose to be blissfully ignorant of what is going on around them.

Endnotes

Goll, Jim W. *The Seer: The Prophetic Power of Visions, Dreams, and Open Heavens.* Shippensburg, PA: Destiny Image Publishers, Inc., 2012

About the Author

Vivienne is a Trauma Specialist bringing wholeness: transforming the human spirit, soul, and body. This is accomplished through being a professionally trained therapist and with Ministry of the Holy Spirit.

In spite being broken by trauma, incest, rape, abortion, domestic violence, bullying, harassment, and mental and emotional abuse, I am a strong, powerful woman of God and more than a conqueror through Him Who loves me: Jesus!

I continue my journey to wholeness by healing the traumas of my spirit, soul, and body through the Ministry of the Holy Spirit and skilled Theophostic counseling as well as looking at the psychological roots and effects of past traumas.

I reside in Port Orange, Florida and serve as an Elder at Fellowship Church of Praise/Volusia County where Drs. Frank and Belinda Watkins are Senior Pastors. I also facilitate a Women's Support Group at FCP/VC Florida.

Awards

Grateful Recognition of Your Outstanding Performance, Productivity and Dedicated Service, November 2002, Serenity House of Volusia, Inc.

For outstanding support to the Volusia County Dependency Drug Court Program. WE THANK YOU.

Healing Trauma, Athens School of Ministry and Worship Arts, Athens, GA.

Education

Perfecting Faith Bible Institute, AS, General Bible, Freeport, NY

Stetson University, Masters of Science, Marriage & Family Therapy, Deland, FL

Fordham University, BA, 18th Century Social History, Bronx, NY

NET Institute, AS, Advanced Addictions Studies, Titusville, FL

Connect with Vivienne

Website: Visit me at Rehoboth555.com
Email: 555rehoboth@gmail.com or VivienneHines@yahoo.com
Facebook: Vivienne Hines
Twitter: AndersonRehoboth

www.ingramcontent.com/pod-product-compliance
Lightning Source LLC
Chambersburg PA
CBHW071427090426
42737CB00011B/1590